The
Chocolate Carousel

A Fun Family Guide to Molding, Modeling and
Creating Magical Gifts from Chocolate

The Chocolate Carousel

A Fun Family Guide to Molding, Modeling and Creating Magical Gifts from Chocolate

Violet Haufsk

Edited by
Lenore Good

Scratch & Scribble Press
Ridge, New York

I will name several products in this book. The names are the copyright or registered trademark of the company that produces them. Doing so does not mean that I am endorsing any one product over another. There are thousands of chocolate products and supplies available. I could not possibly mention them all.

Although the author and publisher have exhaustively researched all sources to ensure the accuracy and completeness of the information contained in this book, we assume no responsibility for errors, inaccuracies, omissions or any other inconsistency herein. Any slights against people or organizations are unintentional. Readers should consult an attorney or accountant for specific applications to their individual candy making ventures.

Edited by Lenore Good
Printed by The Peconic Company, Mattituck, New York
Cover photographs taken by Condé of Diversified Photo Services

Haufsk, Violet.
    The chocolate carousel : a fun family guide to molding, modeling
and creating magical gifts from chocolate / Violet Haufsk ; edited
by Lenore Good. -- 1st ed.
    p. cm.
    Includes index.
    Preassigned LCCN: 97-66381
    ISBN: 0-933675-97-6

    1. Chocolate molds. 2. Chocolate candy.   I. Title.

NK8490.H38 1997   641.6'374
                                   QBI97-40992

Attention Schools, Corporations, and Charitable Organizations: Quantity discounts are available on bulk purchases of this book for educational training purposes, fund raising, or gift giving. Special books, booklets, or book excerpts can also be created to fit your specific needs. For information contact: Marketing Department, Scratch & Scribble Press, Post Office Box 490, Ridge, NY 11961.

For my husband Stephen,
        my munchkins, Jessica, Eddie, Dominick, Stephanie and Samantha
        for without you…there wouldn't be a carousel to ride.

Acknowledgments...

One of the greatest aspects of writing this book was meeting many new and interesting people. In researching the material for The Chocolate Carousel, I encountered so many wonderfully helpful individuals, who not only took the time to speak or meet with me, but sent me great chocolate to taste and sample. What a score! I could not have accomplished this on my own, and would like to take this opportunity to thank you all again.

In fondest memory of Amelia Murphy, a most wonderful lady who took so much time to teach a neophyte about the wonderful makings of chocolate. You will always be remembered for your kindness.

Sheila Heath and The Chocolate Manufacturers Association for all the information they gave me for Chapter 1, The History & Evolution of Chocolate.

Kathy Kempke from the Ambrosia Division of Grace Cocoa, you are a walking encyclopedia and I wish you all the best in your future endeavors.

Gisela Bolte from Albert Uster Imports, Inc.

Kevin Roblee from the Merkens division of Grace Cocoa

Christine Muelter from Blommer

Kathy Rae from Ghirardelli

Colleen Terry from Guittard

Candy from Hawaiian Vintage Chocolate

Malcolm Blue from Peter's Chocolate

Jackie Piché from Van Leer

Amy Buffenmeyer from Wilbur

Barry Krinsky from Life of The Party, some day I will get my toys to New Jersey.

Tim Thil from Tomric Plastics

Kevin from East Coast Mold

Dorothy MacGregor from Classic Design Mold Company

Emily from Emily's Chocolate Store

Kerri and Kevin from Kerrie's Kandies

...and applause

Lenore Good for being a great editor.

My fellow micrographites: Lynn (Mother Superior), Denise (Where's mine), Veronica (Crash), Paul (I want my fifteen minutes of fame) and Ray Amruso (do you really want to be associated with us?) This requires another piece of chocolate, don't you think?

Rosie Horton from Rosie's Cake and Candy Closet, I cherish the day I met you and we became friends. You're the best.

Louise Morante from Classique Creations, my good friend and the only person who understands my enthusiasm for a great piece of clip art.

Michael and Christine Dubritz of Ritz Computers for setting up and putting up with everything from hardware to software and things that go "crash" in the night. Thanks for making sure that I got on line, stayed in line and giving me that "turbo boost" whenever you instinctively knew I needed it.

Denise "Aunt Ni Ni" Miano for just being there... especially in the wee hours of the morning. Who else could I have a conversation with at two or three in the morning.

MariAnn Cole, neighbor, good friend, fellow Disney Maniac, I'll meet you later for canoli.

Mariette Ambra...Sister! Maybe now we can have a cup of tea.

Brenda Teuschler, Sammie and Stephie's "Auntie Brenah" for being the super kid that you are, and being a wonderful friend to my children.

Lynda Hansel, my good friend, you will never know the piece of mind (and I need all the pieces I can get) that you have given me. It is hard enough being a mother, but being a mother who works outside the home is so much easier knowing you are there when I am not.

My mom and Dad for making me believe I could accomplish anything I wanted to do. Here it is.

Stephen, my husband, for giving me my wonderful computer, half of your office space and especially for loving me.

Jessica, Eddie, Dominick, Stephanie and Samantha for making me love cartoons, toys and chocolate. For keeping me young at heart and not letting me take life so serious. I love you too!

PREFACE

As children, we had a sense of magic about life, filled with colorful images and delightful characters...big birds and singing mice; secret gardens and carousels; painted ponies who went round and round in pastel colors, up and down . . .wide eyed and innocent, we marveled over the simple things. Remember when the ice cream man came down the street? His jingle could be heard in the most secretive hiding place, and had every child in the neighborhood scampering to his truck.

Remember the feeling of anticipation you had when you received your first box of chocolates? No? Then close your eyes and picture little finger marks in the bottoms of all the uneaten pieces. Mom had said, "if you bite it you eat it." But she never said anything about sticking your finger into it to take a peak!

Molding and modeling chocolate keeps me on my childhood carousel. Finding the right mold, creating that perfect piece, will conjure up that childhood sense of magic in you, too.

My magical journey with chocolate began many years ago on a day near Easter when a vendor came into the delicatessen which I had been working. He had brought with him the most beautiful handmade chocolates I had ever seen. The bunnies he had were so different from the ones I was used to giving or receiving...his had big round eyes and whimsical expressions that seemed to say, "eat me if you dare." There were ducklings and lambs in pastel colors, and chocolate eggs decorated like the Fabergé eggs in museums. My curiosity was aroused; I set out to find out as much as I could about chocolate-making. More than ten years and five children later, I am still making chocolate.

But chocolate need not only appeal to children. For the child in all of us, homemade chocolate is the ultimate gift—it signifies someone or something special. There always seems to be an occasion calling for something made from chocolate: a shower, birthday, anniversary, retirement, school function, fund raiser, charity, and every holiday imaginable, you name it, and there is a reason to make chocolate.

I truly love molding and modeling chocolate. I've had a lot of fun along the way, and you will, too. Create for your friends and loved ones; create for the child in you. Come take a ride on my carousel. The Chocolate Carousel.

Contents

INTRODUCTION

When you climb on board *The Chocolate Carousel*, you embark on a chocolate journey: one that will take you from wishing you could make magnificent chocolate, to being able to! No matter what your level of skill before reading this book, by following the complete, practical, and easy-to-follow instructions, you will be able to mold picture-perfect chocolate creations that will taste as good as they look.

Your journey will start in the year 1519 with the Emperor Montezuma and the discovery of chocolate. You will travel with Hernando Cortez, the great Spanish explorer, and learn how chocolate evolved into what we know and crave today.

A knowledge of the history, manufacture and types of chocolate will be imperative when it comes time for you to buy, store and melt your chocolate. Learning the basics of chocolate making and the reasons behind the instructions will help you continue your journey and help you gain the confidence you need to create your own chocolate-masterpieces.

Once you've mastered the basics, the journey will continue with sections on techniques; learn to dip succulent strawberries, make tantalizing truffles; create new and exciting garnishes; and enhance your creations with leaves, flowers, lace, and filigree. What could be more impressive than gift wrapping your chocolates in chocolate? You could even tie them with a chocolate ribbon and bow!

Molding chocolate is deceptively easy, and using your new special effects will guarantee many "oohs and ahs!" You will need practice, of course, and patients, to make your mouth-watering array of chocolate creations. I will guide you step-by-step, in a down-to-earth style, sharing all my tips, tricks, and short-cuts learned through years of chocolate making.

We will travel back through time, you and I, remembering our childhood sense of magic...and with all the wonderful things you will have learned, you, too, will be able to build your own carousel.

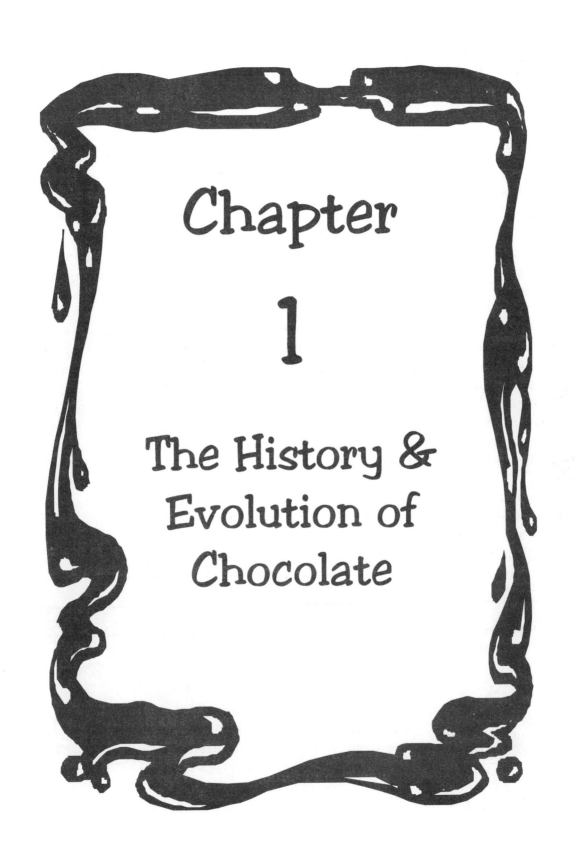

Chapter

1

The History &
Evolution of
Chocolate

Did I Miss This in History 101?

Open the bag of M&Ms . . . History class . . . boring! The Old world, the New World, the great Spanish Explorers, why did I have to learn this stuff? Sneak a few more M&Ms . . .and yes, saved by the bell! Bring back memories?

Perhaps if the teacher included the discovery of chocolate in her curriculum on the Spanish explorers, I would have aced the course, or at the very least provided the class with a decadent display of chocolates for show-and-tell. Hernando Cortez, the great Spanish explorer, was just that, a great Spanish explorer. Little did I know then, that he would command a special place in my heart; for Mr. Cortez was responsible for bringing chocolate to the New World.

The time was 1519. Prior to his conquest of Mexico, Hernando was a guest of Montezuma, Emperor of the Aztecs. Like any good host, the Emperor served his guests his finest and most valued beverage, "chocolatl," meaning warm liquid. The Aztec Indians prepared this drink using roasted cocao beans, which they crushed and mixed with warm water, and served in great golden goblets. Not to offend the Emperor, Hernando and his men drank the beverage even though it was not at all to their liking; Chocolatl, you see, was very bitter.

Hernando was not only adventurous, he was enterprising as well. If something were added to sweeten the chocolatl, he reasoned, it would be a pleasing beverage that his countrymen would like back home. Cane sugar was added and chocolatl was exported to Spain. To enhance its flavor, cinnamon and vanilla was added and the chocolatl beverage was served hot.

Chocolatl became quite popular in Spain, especially in the aristocracy. Realizing the commercial value, the Spanish proceeded to plant cocao in some of their overseas colonies. They were able to keep the art of chocolate making their secret for almost a hundred years; the Spanish monks, who processed the cocao, were the ones who spilled the beans.

Once the secret was out, chocolate quickly found its way through Europe, and in 1657 the first English Chocolate Houses appeared. Chocolate was an expensive beverage, beyond the reach of all but the very wealthy.

The improvements of the steam engine, which ground the cocoa beans, helped bring down the manufacturing costs of chocolate and allowed for its mass-production. In 1728 the first chocolate factory opened in England by the J.S. Fry Company; by 1730 the price of chocolate had dropped dramatically. More and more people were now able to afford to consume chocolate.

While chocolate reigned supreme throughout Europe, its immense popularity with the people of the American Colonies, led to the first chocolate factory being built in New England in 1765; this was and continues to be the home of Baker's Chocolate.

The manufacturing of chocolate made great strides in the 19th Century. In 1828, Conrad Van Houten, a Dutch chemist, invented a hydraulic cocoa press, which squeezed out some of the cocoa butter (a natural fat found in cocoa beans), and improved the quality of the chocolate. Prior to the removal of the cocoa butter, the chocolate drink had a thicker and richer consistency. This new process increased chocolate's popularity and eventually led to the manufacture of cocoa powder.

There were three events that probably had the greatest impact on the chocolate market. First, in 1847, a "solid eating" chocolate was introduced by an English company. This chocolate was smooth in texture, and almost completely replaced its grainy predecessor.

The second dramatic change in the production of chocolate occurred in the seventies. By 1867, the popularity of chocolate had grown to immense proportions, and with it grew competition between manufacturers to create a unique chocolate product. Daniel Peter, a successful chocolate manufacturer, started experimenting with a way to add milk as an ingredient to chocolate. To accomplish this, the water content from the milk had to be removed to prevent mildewing. At the same time, Peter's neighbor, Henri Nestlé, was busy experimenting with milk to be used in his baby food manufacturing company. After working together for more than eight years, Nestlé introduced condensed milk, while Peter, incorporating Nestlé's condensed milk with his chocolate, introduced milk chocolate. Peter and Nestlé found huge success in their individual companies, but even greater success together. One hundred and twenty years later, the Peter's Division of Nestlé's Food Company manufactures and sells a wide variety of fine-quality chocolates.

The third dramatic change in chocolate production came in 1880, when Rodolphe Lindt (another chocolate manufacturer) discovered that "conching" (a method of kneading the chocolate mass at a set temperature for a specific period of time) resulted in a smoother and better flavored chocolate.

As technology advanced, so did the production of chocolate. New and better methods of manufacturing were developed and the result is that there are chocoholics on every continent. Today chocolate is found in every corner of the earth; the astronauts have even taken it into outer space. It has literally grown from a bean to a billion-dollar industry.

Chocolatl To Chocolate

Cocao beans are the product of the cocao tree, *Theobroma cacao, L.* Theobroma is a Greek word meaning "food of the gods;" cocao comes from the Aztec "cacahuatl;" and the L. stands for Linnaeus, the Swedish botanist who classified it under that name.

The cocao tree grows in moist tropical countries not more than 20 degrees north or south of the equator. African countries harvest two-thirds of the total world output of cocoa: Ghana, Côte d´lvoire, Nigeria, and Cameroon are the leading African cocao producers. The remaining cocao trees are cultivated in Central and South America, the West Indies, and parts of Asia. In 1986, the first cocao trees were planted on American soil. Jim Walsh, the founder and President of Hawaiian Vintage Chocolate, is successfully growing and manufacturing America's only home-grown chocolate on the island of Hawaii.

The cocao tree is a beautiful 15 to 25-foot tall evergreen with large shiny red leaves which turn green when mature; it has thousands of clusters of tiny white or pink flowers which form on its trunk and older branches. Only about 10 percent of these flowers will mature into full fruit, and eventually be turned into chocolate. (Now when the kids are eating chocolate like it is going out of style, you won't be able to say "what do you think, chocolate grows on trees?" Now you know it does!!)

There are many different types of cocao trees due to cross-pollination; however, they are classified into three main types. The Criollo, the king of cocaos, is used to make the finest chocolates. It is light-colored, with a thin pod and pleasant aroma. The second type, Forastero, is the most widely cultivated type. It is somewhat easier to grow and has a high yield. It has a thick-walled shell and a pungent aroma. The Trinitario, the third type, is a cross between the Criollo and Forastero.

No matter what the variety, all cocao trees grow in the same way. The fruit, or cocao pods, grow right from the trunk or the large branches near the trunk. They are mainly green or maroon in color and look like elongated melons, tapered at both ends. They grow from six to fourteen inches long and two to five inches in diameter. The hard shelled pods contain anywhere from 20 to 50 cocao beans enclosed within an inner membrane and are surrounded by a layer of gummy, gelatinous pulp.

Harvesting the cocao pods is not an easy task. Since the growing season in the tropics is year round, the trained and experienced pickers have to determine which pods are ripe for cutting by appearance. Because the cocao tree is too fragile to bear the weight of the picker, they must cut the pods standing on the ground with long handled sharp knives.

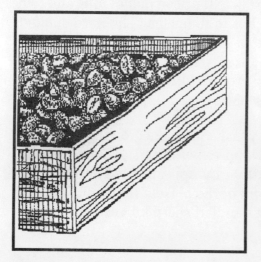

The pods are then gathered and brought to the edge of the growing field where the pod breaking operation begins. An experienced breaker and his machete can open 500 pods an hour. (I break out in a sweat just thinking about it.) The beans and surrounding pulp are scooped out of the hard shells and are then readied for fermentation.

The fermentation process is a natural chemical reaction. Due to oxidation, the beans which are creamy-white in the pod, turn a lavender purple shortly upon being exposed to the air. The beans and their surrounding pulp are put in boxes or heaps from three to nine days. The natural sugars in the pulp convert into acids, primarily lactic and acetic, generating temperatures up to 125° F. The fermentation period removes the raw bitter taste and creates essential oils, which will give the beans their chocolate flavor when they are roasted. The beans are then air dried for several days to remove most of their moisture; this is very important otherwise molds would develop on the beans giving them an irreversible unfavorable flavor.

The cocoa beans, now resembling a cross between coffee beans and pistachio nuts, are then put in bags and shipped to the Cocoa Exchanges (similar to stock exchanges). The manufacturers can now buy their beans and the magic can begin.

Cocao to Cocoa

What a wonderful thing, if the change from the cocao bean to the chocolate bar was as easy as changing the word cocao to cocoa. While reading the history and growing of the bean you probably thought we had some spelling errors there. " Cocao," explained earlier, comes from the botanical name, *Theobroma cacao, L.*; it refers to the tree, pod, and the unfermented beans. "Cocoa," refers to the manufactured products from the fermented bean.

Your next stop on The Chocolate Carousel takes you to the manufacturing plant. It is there that you will experience the true magic that transforms the cocoa bean to the chocolate that we know and love. The selection of cocoa beans used in the production of chocolate is unique to each individual chocolate manufacturer; their unique blend of beans, flavorings, and treatments is what distinguishes one chocolate from another. Even though their methods differ in detail from plant to plant, a fundamental system regulated by the Food and Drug Administration must be followed.

When the cocoa beans arrive at the plant, each shipment is inspected, tested (quality control is strictly adhered to), and then catalogued according to its particular type and origin. This enables the chocolate maker to maintain exact control over the flavor blending of the beans and ensures the production of uniformly high quality chocolate.

The first step in the manufacturing process is cleaning. The beans are put into machines which contain special components that remove any foreign matter; any remaining traces of twigs, dirt, pod or dried pulp which may not have been removed prior to shipping are removed at this point.

Like a master chef preparing one of his famous dishes, the skilled chocolate maker selects his blend of beans according to his own unique recipe and deposits them into a roasting machine. The beans are then roasted from thirty minutes to two hours at temperatures ranging from 230°-300° F. The differences between the quality and types of chocolate result from these variations in time and temperature.

Cocoa beans can not develop their flavor, aroma or rich brown color until they have been slowly roasted. During roasting, the heat must be evenly distributed throughout the bean, making sure not to burn the bean's outer shell.

The outer shell is loosened by this roasting process. It must be removed in order to get to the heart of the bean, or the "nib;" the nib is the chocolate. The roasted beans are placed into a winnowing machine; the machines are equipped with "impact" rollers which crack the shells, then pass them through a series of sieves where the shell and nib are separated by currents of air. The shells are discarded, while the nibs remain.

The nibs contain an average of 53 percent cocoa butter; they are composed of cells, with the cocoa fat in solid form. They are ground between large heavy stones or steel discs, which causes the nibs to rupture. The heat produced by the grinding discs causes the now-released cocoa butter to liquefy. This thick dark paste, consisting of small particles of cocoa nib suspended in fluid cocoa butter, is called chocolate liquor. Chocolate liquor is non-alcoholic; the term refers merely to the chocolate in its liquid state. When this liquid cools and hardens, it becomes what we know as unsweetened chocolate, a staple in our baking.

The Food and Drug Administration (FDA) sets standard for all chocolate products. The FDA defines and regulates what can be added and removed from chocolate. Chocolate liquor contains between 53 and 55 percent cocoa butter, just like the nibs from which it was made. The FDA allows the manufacturers to adjust the content of the cocoa butter, but it must remain between 50 and 60 percent. Further reduction, or additions of cocoa butter to the chocolate liquor make either cocoa powder or eating chocolate.

Cocoa Powder

Remember chocolatl, the beverage the Aztecs made by crushing the roasted cocoa beans back in 1519? We said the drink was bitter, thick, and very rich; now we can understand why. Chocolatl was made from a crude form of chocolate liquor. Remember how the invention of the cocoa press increased the popularity of the chocolate drink? The removal of some of the cocoa butter reduced the fat content, producing a smoother drink.

Today, cocoa powder is made by further removing the remaining cocoa butter from the chocolate liquor. The manufacturer pours the chocolate liquor into a press and literally squeezes out most of the cocoa butter fat. What remains is a dry, solid cocoa cake which is then pulverized into a fine, cocoa powder. The cocoa butter which had been extracted is used in both the manufacturing of eating chocolate and in the cosmetic industry.

Cocoa powder may be "natural" or "Dutch" processed. Remember Mr. Van Houten, the Dutch chemist who invented the cocoa press? Well he also devised a way to improve the flavor and color of cocoa powder. By treating the nibs, chocolate liquor or cocoa powder with an alkali solution (usually potassium bicarbonate) a stronger flavord cocoa powder is produced having a darker color.

The FDA classifies cocoa powder according to its fat content. There are three grades: breakfast cocoa, or high fat cocoa, contains at least 22 percent fat content; cocoa, or medium fat cocoa, contains at least 10 percent but no more than 22 percent fat content; and low-fat, contains less than a 10 percent fat content.

Cocoa Butter

It is important to understand the effect cocoa butter has in chocolate making, and how it could effect your creation. An explanation here will undoubtedly lead to fewer frustrations later in the kitchen.

Cocoa butter is the natural vegetable fat from the cocoa bean. Unlike most vegetable fats, it stays solid at room temperature. Cocoa butter's melting point is between 89°-93° F., just below normal body temperature. The higher the cocoa butter content in the chocolate you use, the more melt-in-your-mouth quality it has. Cocoa butter is what gives chocolate its shine, creaminess, and crisp snap when it's broken. Molding chocolate into chips, bars and artistic shapes is possible because of cocoa butter's ability to contract (reduce in size) when it solidifies.

With all its wonderful attributes, though, there is one catch; cocoa butter is polymorphic. This means it has the ability to assume several forms because its natural makeup is comprised of several different fatty acids. This in itself is not an altogether bad thing, but each type of fatty acid melts and solidifies at a different temperature. Chocolate manufacturers use a technique called "tempering" (more on this topic later) to force all the fatty acids in the cocoa butter to take the same solid form. If tempering were not done, the final chocolate product would be dull, crumbly and have grayish white streaks (bloom) on its surface.

Chocolate Liquor

As a child, my mother always baked, especially around the holidays. Entering our house, guests were immediately struck by the rich aroma of Mom's freshly baked cookies. Following the wonderful scent, their eyes would feast upon a dining room table covered with pile after delicious pile of cookies, all lovingly prepared for friends and family.

Naturally, Mom kept a variety of chocolate in the cupboard to use in making these delightful treats; cocoa powder, baking chocolate, and chocolate chips were staples in her kitchen. I received my first lesson in the differences between chocolates when I snuck some baking chocolate from the counter and popped it into my mouth. I thought I had pulled one over on Mom, but she had the last laugh when she heard my mournful yuck!!, as I sank my teeth into the huge chunk of baking chocolate.

Baking chocolate, as we discussed earlier, is chocolate liquor in solid form, unsweetened, hard and not quite melt-in-your-mouth quality. To make chocolate more pleasing to the palate, extra cocoa butter must be added to the chocolate liquor to lower its viscosity (making it thinner and more fluid). Depending on which type of chocolate is desired, various amounts of sugar, flavorings and/or milk products are added to the chocolate liquor and mixed together according to recipes known only to the chocolate makers themselves.

Refining

The mixed chocolate at this point has the consistency of a doughy-paste. It is put into a refining machine which pulverizes the mixture. The sugar and cocoa particles are ground smaller and finer until the desired texture is obtained.

Conching

The now-refined chocolate paste is transferred to a "conching" machine, which kneads the chocolate back and forth and creates an even smoother texture; the agitation and aeration ensure perfect flavor development. Any particles which somehow managed to escape grinding in the refining process are broken up in the conching process. To achieve the desired texture and flavor, the conching process can be anywhere from a few hours to as many as several days. The result is a velvety-smooth, perfectly flavored liquid chocolate; it must then be tempered to form that shiny, snap-when-you-break-it, chocolate bar we love to indulge in.

Tempering

Tempering is the technique used to force the different types of fatty acids present in the cocoa butter to crystallize properly (solidify all at the same time). We already know that cocoa butter is polymorphic. The four common fatty acids in cocoa butter affecting its crystallization are named by letters of the Greek alphabet: gamma, alpha, beta-prime and beta. The objective of tempering is to have the chocolate crystallize in the beta form. To accomplish this, the chocolate is heated and cooled and heated again at specific temperatures. The chocolate leaves the manufacturing plant in a good tempered state. When you re-melt the chocolate to use it in your chocolate creations, the chocolate comes out of temper and must be tempered again. Now this may seem a bit intimidating, but, do not worry…you will learn several different methods of hand tempering, and even be given a fail-safe alternative.

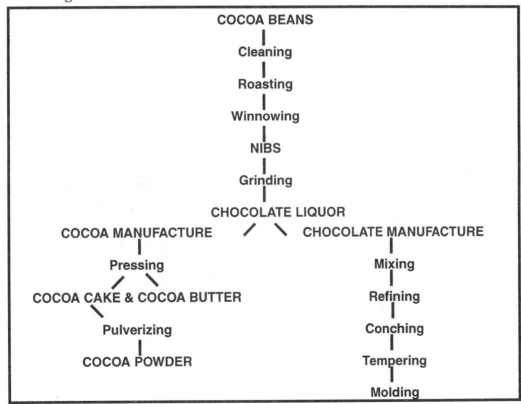

```
                         COCOA BEANS
                              |
                           Cleaning
                              |
                           Roasting
                              |
                          Winnowing
                              |
                             NIBS
                              |
                           Grinding
                              |
                      CHOCOLATE LIQUOR
   COCOA MANUFACTURE        /   \        CHOCOLATE MANUFACTURE
             |                                      |
          Pressing                               Mixing
          /   \                                     |
 COCOA CAKE & COCOA BUTTER                       Refining
          \                                         |
        Pulverizing                              Conching
             |                                      |
       COCOA POWDER                             Tempering
                                                    |
                                                 Molding
```

How We Define Chocolate

Deciding which type of chocolate to use in your projects should not be a stressful or difficult decision to make. On the contrary, it should be an exciting experience, a time when you can taste and experiment with many varieties of chocolate—a guilt-free chocolate splurge! I know what you are thinking...is she crazy? There are thousands of chocolates to choose from!! Naturally, I would not expect you to purchase and try every available type (talk about *death by chocolate*!), but being an educated consumer would definitely narrow the field.

There are literally thousands of candy makers in the United States, but only fourteen actually manufacture their chocolate from the bean to the chocolate bar. Out of these fourteen, less than a dozen manufactures chocolate in bulk for use in the confectionery trade and for chocolatiers like us. There are also several popular brands of imported chocolates that are readily available from specialty shops and candy supply stores. The chocolate and chocolate-like products that these companies manufacture are generally grouped into three categories: chocolate (chocolate coating), white confectioner's coating, and compound coatings.

More often than not, you will encounter the term "real" chocolate or "true" chocolate in chocolate discussions. I hate this! Aside from being confusing and misleading, it sends a negative connotation that a chocolate-like product, being "un-real" or "untrue" is inferior or substandard. Nonsense! Chocolate is chocolate is chocolate. The Food and Drug Administration defines chocolate. In order for a product in the United States to be labeled chocolate, it has to contain chocolate liquor and cocoa butter. So it stands to reason, that if the product does not contain chocolate liquor or cocoa butter, it is something other than chocolate. Therefore, since white confectioner's coatings and compound coatings don't contain these essential ingredients, they are categories into themselves. Not by any stretch of the imagination are they inferior, just different.

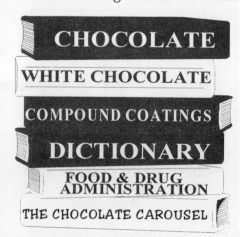

White Confectioner's Coating

White confectioner's coating is what most European countries have named "white chocolate." It is a product made from cocoa butter, milk solids, sugar and flavorings. Since there is no chocolate liquor added to this product, it cannot be labeled "white chocolate" in the United States as per the FDA's standards of identity.

Chocolates

Unsweetened, Sweet, Semi-sweet and Milk chocolate are types of chocolate. To ensure uniform labeling and ingredients, the FDA has set standards to identify each one. Each type contains a specified amount of chocolate liquor and cocoa butter. Most manufacturers produce a variety of each type, geared to specific uses. The following are the ingredients commonly found in the manufacture of chocolate and white confectioner's coating:

Sugar, of a very high grade, which has gone through a refining process to eliminate any moisture content.

Cocoa Butter, extracted from the cocoa powder process, is added in varying amounts to the different types of chocolate and white confectioner's coating. The higher amount of cocoa butter content the chocolate or coating has, the lower it's viscosity (more fluid).

Milk Solids and Milk Fats are added if the desired product is milk chocolate. They are added as evaporated milk in a dry powder form, or as milk crumb, which is a dried mixture of evaporated milk and sugar.

Butter Oil, which is dehydrated unsalted dairy butter, is used as an anti-bloom agent. Added to the chocolate, it helps prevent the cocoa butter from morphing out and creating grayish white streaks on your candies.

Emulsifiers are surface-active agents used to stabilize an emulsion (they keep fat products from separating). The most common one used in chocolate is lecithin, which is a nutritious, natural matter found in all living things. Soya lecithin, which comes from soya beans (the most popular kind), lowers the viscosity of the chocolate (thins it) and serves to lower the amount of cocoa butter that might ordinarily be required to keep the chocolate soft and flexible.

Flavorings originate from the blend of cocoa beans used and the caramelization of the milk products (in milk chocolate), but can be further enhanced by the addition of natural and artificial flavorings. Vanilla and vanillin (artificial vanilla) are the most common; cinnamon and the essential oils of almond, orange and lemon are also frequently added.

Artificial Sweeteners in the form of Sorbitol, Xylitol, Maltitol, and Mannitol are used in the manufacture of dietetic chocolates. It should be noted that extra fats and proteins are usually added to dietetic chocolates to replace the bulk normally occupied by the sugar. Dietetic chocolates are for sugar-restricted diets and should not be mistaken for a less fattening treat.

CHOCOLATE LIQUOR, as we discussed earlier, is the fluid mass of cocoa nib particles suspended in the cocoa butter. It is the foundation which all chocolate is built.

UNSWEETENED CHOCOLATE, or baking chocolate, as it is commonly known, is 100 percent chocolate liquor in its solid form. It is the purest of all chocolate; bitter in taste, since no sugar is added. The FDA requires that it contain no less than 50 percent cocoa fats and no more than 60 percent cocoa fats.

SWEET CHOCOLATE is a combination of at least 15 percent chocolate liquor, additional cocoa butter and sugar; it must also contain less than 12 percent milk solids.

SEMI-SWEET AND BITTERSWEET, as far as the FDA is concerned, are one and the same. They are made from a combination of unsweetened chocolate, cocoa butter, sugar and flavorings. They must contain a minimum of 35 percent chocolate liquor, but can contain up to 60 percent. Do not assume that semi-sweet will be sweeter than bittersweet, since the amount of chocolate liquor, cocoa butter and sugar contained in this type of chocolate can vary so much from brand to brand, one company's bittersweet could be sweeter than another company's semi-sweet.

MILK CHOCOLATE is a combination of chocolate liquor (at least 10 percent), sugar, milk solids (at least 12 percent), milk fats (at least 3.66 percent) and flavorings.

Compound Coatings

Compound coatings are sometimes referred to as "alternatives" to chocolate or white confectioner's coating. They are made from a combination of chocolate liquor or cocoa, sugar, milk (for milk chocolate-like coating) and flavorings. They contain no cocoa butter, the manufacturer substitutes a specially selected vegetable fat for the cocoa butter. Some common names for compound coatings are rainbow wafers, pastels, molding chocolate, summer coating, smooth-'n-melty, and confectioner's chocolate (do not mistake this for white confectioner's coating made with cocoa butter). Read the ingredient label carefully! Since there is no cocoa butter in compound coatings, you do not need to temper it. You (as Guittard so aptly named one of their brands of compound coating) Melt'n Mold™. The ingredients used in compound coatings are similar to the ones used in chocolate; the main difference between them are the vegetable fats, which are broken in two categories.

Lauric Fats, usually in the form of palm kernel oil and coconut oils are used in compound coatings. They are not polymorphic, so tempering is not needed when you use this type of coating for molding. It should be noted that lauric fat-based coatings are not compatible with cocoa butter. They do not mix well. You will get bloom on your creation if you mix the two products.

Non-Lauric Fats, usually in the form of Kaomel (made from soybean and cottonseed oils), are also used in compound coatings. These fats are not polymorphic and also do not need to be tempered. This type of coating is compatible with cocoa butter and can be used in conjunction with chocolate or white confectioner's coatings.

Low Fat Cocoa is used in the chocolate-flavored coatings. Since the lauric fats are not compatible with cocoa butter, the fat content in the cocoa must be low enough (about 9-11 percent) to prevent bloom from appearing on the coating.

Nonfat Milk powder is used in compound coatings. It is used in greater proportions in non-chocolate flavored varieties.

Sugar, which is pulverized for coating manufacturing, is of a high grade and low moisture content.

Emulsifiers may be used to control viscosity and produce a glossier finish.

Flavorings of many varieties are used in compound coatings; while cocoa and chocolate liquor flavor the chocolate-like coatings, vanilla, mint, peanut butter, hazelnut, and an endless assortment of fruit flavors are also frequently used.

Colors are readily available to coordinate your coatings with holidays and other special occasions.

Chapter

2

So Many Choices

Decisions ... Decisions ...

There are several things to consider when choosing which type of chocolate or chocolate-like product you will be using. Oftentimes you will meet someone who is a staunch advocate of chocolate and is vehemently opposed to the use of compound coatings. I myself have been in many a heated debate over the virtues of both. I personally use compound coatings in most of my chocolate creations and have for years. I also use chocolate and an enormous quantity of white confectioner's coating. Taste, cost, availability, experience and the desired end-result of your work, are all factors to take into consideration before buying or molding anything.

Taste is a matter of personal preference, just like coffee or wine. What tastes good to one person may be appalling to another. White confectioner's coating is usually sweeter than chocolate. Imported chocolate usually has a smoother feel in your mouth than chocolate made in America (due to the longer conching times preferred by European manufacturers). Some people argue that chocolate has a richer taste than compound coating. When I was experimenting with different brands of chocolate and compound coatings, I had many informal taste tests among friends; they were not told what they were eating—chocolate or compound coatings—they were just told to eat. Suffice it to say, a good compound coating was overwhelmingly preferred to an expensive chocolate. I am not implying that compound coatings are equal to chocolate; just do not assume that because it's chocolate, it's guaranteed to taste better.

Cost unfortunately, is a reality we all have to live with. It is not always true that the higher the price, the finer the quality. Chocolate and white confectioner's coating are more expensive than compound coatings. Imported is usually more costly than domestic. The price you pay may differ depending on the store in which you make your purchase, and the location of that store. (Rents, for example vary greatly, and the higher costs will be passed down, unfortunately, to the consumer.) If you are making a gift for someone, there is nothing sweeter than creating it from an imported chocolate that they love, or normally wouldn't buy. However, if you are making fifty lollipops in the shape of a dinosaur, for a two year olds birthday, the child's mother may not want to pay the extra money it would cost to use chocolate over compound coating.

Availability may be a problem to folks who live in certain areas. If the products you are looking for are not available, or if no candy supply store exists in your area, items can be directly shipped to your home. When buying products by mail, it is important to keep in mind that many companies have a minimum quantity they will ship, and some companies will not ship chocolate at all during the hot summer months. I have become very friendly with my suppliers and have a wonderful working relationship with them. There is a store here on Long Island, *Rosie's Cake and Candy Closet,* that I have been going to for years. The owner, Rosie Horton, has become a close friend and someone I can call on for almost anything. If she doesn't carry it in her store, she knows where to get it. A good solid relationship with your neighborhood candy store is a valuable asset, and one that can not be emphasized enough.

Experience is something you acquire through time and patience. Compound coatings tend to be easier to work with because they do not have to be tempered the way chocolate and white confectioner's coating do. You may want to try working with compound coatings in the beginning and ease your way into chocolate, or you may be very happy staying with compound coatings exclusively.

Your desired end result has a lot to do with the type of product you use. In the manufacturing process, we discussed how the different blends of beans, flavorings, amount of cocoa butter and chocolate liquor all contribute to the flavor of the final product; some varieties of chocolate, as well as compound coatings, are specifically geared to compliment or enhance other ingredients you may be using.

The Choice is Yours

Unless they have a retail outlet, most manufacturers use a distributor to sell their products. That is because they have minimum quantity requirements—usually five hundred pounds. For those of us who do not need that amount, we must find a store or specialty shop that carries what we want. Most stores break up cases, and purchases as small as one pound are available. If you do not have a store near by, call the manufacturer and ask for a distributor or specialty store that carries their products in your area. The names and addresses of the manufacturers can be found in the reference section towards the end of this book.

The following list of manufacturers and types of products they sell is not a complete list—that would be another book. But this list will give you an overall idea of what choices you have. As I said earlier, what chocolate or chocolate-like product you ultimately decide to use is purely a matter of personal preference. With this in mind _The descriptions of the different products are the descriptions used by the individual manufacturers to describe their products._ Sample, experiment, sample, have fun, and then sample some more. It is the only way to discover what works best for you and what you like best.

Compound Coatings

AMBROSIA-NON-TEMPERING COATINGS-In 10 pound blocks

Non-Tempering Dark Chocolate Flavored Coating
An easy-to-use non-tempering coating with a taste like bittersweet chocolate.
- Melt to coat candies, cookies, pretzels, petit fours.
- Use to decorate and design cakes and tortes.
- Use to make molded candies.
- Use for easy almond or raisin bark.

Non-Tempering Milk Chocolate Flavored Coating
A smooth milk chocolate flavored coating. Easy to use.
- Melt to coat cakes, cheesecakes, and pound cakes.
- Shave and curl for cake decorating.
- Use to make molded candies.
- Use for easy almond bark.

Non-Tempering Pearl White Coating
A creamy white coating for those who want the mystique of "white coating" without the trouble of tempering.
- Melt to coat candies, fruit, cookies, pretzels.
- Use for fondue dipping.
- Use to decorate and design desserts.
- Melt and add nuts or dried fruits to create almond bark.

AMBROSIA® COMPOUND COATINGS-Button shaped comes in 50 pound case
- Pearl White™- A versatile creamy white coating with a predominantly vanilla flavor.
- Landmark™- A well-rounded milk chocolate flavored coating.
- Choice Blend™- A very sweet milk chocolate flavored coating.
- Coronado- A well-rounded dark chocolate flavored coating.
- Milk Chocolate Flavored Sucrose Free™- A smooth milk chocolate coating for sucrose-restricted diets.

BLOMMER CONFECTIONER COATINGS-50 pound cartons

Blommer has lauric fat based and non-lauric fat based coatings. Their K-Dark and K-Lite coatings are made with Kaomel. These can be used with cocoa butter products. All their products are certified kosher.

- Riviera- Their highest quality milk chocolate confectioner coating.
- Target- Their most popular milk chocolate confectioner coating.
- K-Lite- A non-tempering milk chocolate confectioner coating.
- Wyoming- A higher melting point milk chocolate confectioner coating.
- Football- A milk chocolate confectioner coating.
- Montana- A thin milk flavored cocoa confectioner coating.
- Colorado- A confectioner's coating sweetened with buttermilk powder and barley malt powder.
- Morocco- A high quality dark chocolate confectionery coating.
- Target Dark- A high quality dark chocolate confectioner coating.
- Eclipse- A high quality dark chocolate confectioner coating.
- K-Dark- A non-tempering dark chocolate confectioner coating.
- Hawaii- A unique confectioner's coating using a small amount of chocolate liquor for a chocolate impact.

BLOMMER KREEMY PASTEL COATINGS-50 pound cartons

Pastel coatings that have a silky smooth texture and a creamy rich flavor.

- Kreemy White
- Kreemy Pink
- Kreemy Green
- Kreemy Yellow

BLOMMER "SUCROSE FREE" COATINGS

- Maltitol Milk
- Mannitol Milk
- Mannitol White

BLOMMER "SUGAR FREE" COATING

- Maltitol Sugar Free Milk
- Maltitol Dark
- Mannitol Dark

CACAO BARRY (French Import) available in 9 pound cans

These coatings come in a can (P.A.G. which stands for *Pate A Glacer*) that you submerge in a *bain marie* (hot-water bath) and melt. You dip and work straight from the container it comes in.

- Brune Dipping Chocolate Coating (Dark)
- Blonde Dipping Chocolate Coating (Milk)
- Cafe Dipping Chocolate Coating (Coffee)
- Noisette Dipping Chocolate Coating (Hazelnut)

CARMA CHOCOLATE GLAZES (Swiss Import)-13¼ pound blocks

All Carma Glazes are perfect for dipping, coating fruits, cakes, cookies, & candies.Use your creativity! Hard glazes are ideal for any type of molding and for use in warm climates.

- Original Milk Glaze
- Original Vanilla Glaze, semisweet
- Original Hazelnut Glaze
- Mocca Glaze
- White Glaze
- Hard Milk Chocolate Glaze
- Hard Dark Chocolate Glaze
- Blanca Hard White Chocolate Glaze

CARMA COINS (Swiss Import)-Packaged in 17.6 pound boxes-two to a case (35.2 pounds)

- Original Vanilla Glaze, semisweet
- Original Milk Glaze
- White Glaze

CARMA CHOPPED GLAZE (Swiss Import)-44 pounds per case

- Swiss Line Nova, dark chopped chocolate (vanilla) glaze.

GUITTARD PASTEL COATINGS in 50 pound case or 10 pound blocks

These coatings are in the form of ribbons, shaped in thin, flat strips for easy handling and melting. Ideal for molding, and decorating, and recommended for dipping candy, cookies, fruit, cake pieces and for fondue use.They harden to a superior glossy appearance. They are vanilla flavored and colored and one is colored and flavored butterscotch.

- White Pastel Coating
- Butterscotch Coating
- Green Pastel Coating
- Pink Pastel Coating
- Yellow Pastel Coating
- Creamy White Coating
- White Satin Coating
- Yogurt Coating

GUITTARD A'PEELS - FRUIT & CHOCOLATE FLAVORED COATINGS
25 pound case

A'Peels are kiss shaped drops, brightly colored and flavored.They are great for dipping, molding, decorating or for use as fondue dip.

- Lemon A'Peels
- Orange A'Peels
- Strawberry A'Peels
- Vanilla A'Peels
- Lite Chocolate Flavored A'Peels
- Dark Chocolate Flavored A'Peels
- Green Mint A'Peels

- Red Vanilla Flavored A'Peels
- Red Mint A'Peels

GUITTARD MELT'n MOLD 16 ounce bag

Due to the growing popularity of home candy making, Guittard has taken their quality coatings and conveniently packaged them in 16 ounce bags. Available in eight vibrant colors and eight luscious flavors.

- Dark Chocolate
- Milk Chocolate
- Mint Chocolate
- Vanilla
- Lemon
- Orange
- Strawberry
- Green Mint

MERCKENS RAINBOW CHOCOLATE FLAVORED AND PASTEL COATINGS

These coatings are made from cocoa powder and vegetable oil. They have a low working temperature which makes them easy and flexible to use for enrobing and molding. These wafer shaped coatings are excellent for dipping and rolling fruits and nuts, or piping as decoration.

- Rainbow Cocoa Dark- A vanilla chocolate flavored coating.
- Rainbow Cocoalite- A rich milk chocolate flavored coating.
- Rainbow White- A rich, creamy vanilla-like flavor. Silky texture and easy handling.
- Rainbow Red- A red version of Rainbow White.
- Rainbow Blue- A blue version of Rainbow White.
- Rainbow Peach- A peach version of Rainbow White.
- Rainbow Green- A green version of Rainbow White.
- Rainbow Pink- A pink version of Rainbow White.
- Rainbow Yellow- A yellow version of Rainbow White.
- Rainbow Orange- An orange version of Rainbow White.
- Rainbow Dark Green- A dark green version of Rainbow White.
- Rainbow Orchid- An orchid version of Rainbow White.
- Rainbow Peanut butter- A peanut butter flavored coating.
- Rainbow Butterscotch- A butterscotch flavored coating.

NESTLÉ ICECAP CONFECTIONARY COATINGS- packed in five 10-pound blocks per case

Are good for hand dipping or molding with good enrobing characteristics.

- Westchester- A milk chocolate-flavored coating, frequently used in molded items. Also used as a bottom coating.
- Eastchester- A semisweet chocolate-flavored medium dark coating. Used in a wide variety of bakery applications.
- White Icecap- The basic pastel coating. Can be used as is or colored and/or flavored with oil based products.

NESTLÉ ICECAP CAPS -packed 25 pounds net per case

Nestlé Icecap caps are lower-viscosity versions of their block Icecap products. The white and colored Caps all have a mild vanilla flavor and are made in handy button-shaped form for easy melting and molding. They come in pink, white, Westchester, Eastchester, green, yellow, red, Holiday green, orange, blue and natural peanut-flavored caps.

VAN LEER COMPOUND COATINGS-30 pound cases

These compound coatings come in round discs called "snaps". They are great for molding and garnishing. Available in milk, dark, white, and peanut butter flavors and pink, green, holiday green, yellow, blue, red, orange, lavender, and peach colored versions of the white.

VAN LEER COMPOUND SLABS-50 pound cases with five 10-pound bars

These coatings are recommended for candy making and bottoming.
- Milkcote
- Darkcote

VAN LEER BOTTOMCOTE-50 pound cases with five 10-pound bars

These coatings are recommended to use as bottom for centers.
- Dark Bottomcote N Slabs
- Light Bottomcote

WILBUR

Wilbur offers one of the most diverse lines of confectionery products available. The following is just a sampling of some of their most popular products.
- F-497- A sweet, milky-flavored coating made with lauric fat.
- H-282- The flavor of milk chocolate with a slightly stronger vanilla note. Made with lauric fat.
- H-301- A milk chocolate-like coating made with lauric fat.
- H-449- Their very best milk chocolate-like confectionery coating with a creamy rich flavor. Made with lauric fat.
- N-254 Undercoat- A product formulated specifically to function as a bottomer for chocolate enrobing. Made with non-lauric fat.
- #37 Darkcoat (Parve)- A popular choice in bakery use, this quality dark confectionery coating is made with a high melt-point vegetable oil. Made with lauric fat.
- D-704- A competitively priced, dark confectionery coating suitable for enrobing cookies and cake products where a thin coating is desired. Made with lauric fat.
- H-472- Their highest quality dark confectionery coating with a pleasant flavor reminiscent of sweet vanilla chocolate. Made with lauric fat.
- D-858- A slightly stronger chocolate flavored product, containing some chocolate liquor. Ideal for enrobing bakery products. Made with non-lauric fat

- • H-396-Butterscotch Coating- Delivers a distinct butterscotch flavor. Made with lauric fat.
- • K-886-Fiesta White Coating- Their best quality white confectionery coating with improved handling. Made with lauric fat.

WILBUR PASTEL CONFECTIONERY COATINGS
These high quality pastel coatings are made with lauric fats.
- • Sunlight White
- • Sunlight Pink
- • Sunlight Yellow
- • Sunlight Green
- • Sunlight Orange

WILBUR CONFECTIONERY WAFER
Their most popular confectionery coatings are available in wafer form. All are made with lauric fat.
- • Milk Chocolate Flavored Confectionery
- • Dark Chocolate Flavored Confectionery
- • White Confectionery
- • Peanut Butter-Flavored Confectionery

WILTON CANDY MELTS® CONFECTIONERY COATING-packaged in 14 ounce bags.
Easy-to-melt wafers ideal for molding, dipping, and coating. Certified Kosher.
- • Chocolate-Flavored- Dark Cocoa, Light Cocoa.
- • Vanilla-Flavored- white, pink, yellow, light green, Christmas Mix (red and green), Pastel Mix (pink, lavender & blue), orange, and red.
- • Mint Flavored-Chocolate Mint, Pastel Mint (pink, green & white).

Domestic Chocolate and White Confectioner's Coating

AMBROSIA
Chocolate Liquor
The high cocoa butter content gives it a rich, smooth consistency.
- • Ambrosia Reliance- A naturally processed quality liquor.
- • Ambrosia Tropic Crushed- A crushed, dutched liquor with a milder taste and darker color than natural liquors.

Elite Bittersweet Chocolate Couverture/Coating
Their finest pure dark chocolate Couverture Coating.
- • Temper and melt to dip fruit, pretzels, cookies and candy.
- • Chunk and add to gourmet-type cookies and brownies.
- • Use to make frostings, puddings, fillings.
- • Shave for decorating desserts.
- • Melt for upscale fondue.

Prestige Milk Chocolate Couverture/Coating
Pure milk chocolate with its milder and sweeter taste, is ideal for pies and tortes. Suitable for confections too.
- Temper and melt to dip cookies, pretzels, chips, fruit.
- Shave to decorate desserts.
- Create a milk chocolate fondue.

Empress White Cocoa Butter Couverture/Coating
With its creamy cocoa butter base, this premium coating is excellent as a dessert garnish or in molded sweets. Known as "white chocolate" in Europe.
- Use to make frostings and decorations for wedding cakes.
- Melt to dip fruit, pretzels, cookies, nuts.
- Add to batters for cheesecakes, brownies, cookies and cakes.
- Use to marbleize brownies, cakes and pies.

BLOMMERS

Chocolate Liquor
- Special- Their finest chocolate liquor formulated with a select blend of flavor-grade cocoa beans that are carefully roasted to create a unique flavor.
- Standard- Their most popular chocolate liquor.

Dark Chocolate
- New York Imperial- Their finest dark chocolate made with gently roasted cocoa beans. It is then carefully refined and conched to create a silky smooth texture.
- Sierra- A high quality dark chocolate with a pleasant chocolate flavor. Distinguished by its richness.
- Coronet- A bold dark chocolate manufactured with a full roast to create a strong chocolate impact.
- Alamo- One of their finest dark chocolates, using a unique blend of flavor-grade beans that has been lightly dutched.
- Chesapeake-A premium dark chocolate blend of flavor-grade beans with subtle fruity notes.
- D-2- A bold dark chocolate manufactured with a full roast to create a strong chocolate impact.
- Columbia- A dark chocolate using specially roasted cocoa beans to create a rich chocolate flavor.
- Kirmess- A fine dark chocolate with a mild chocolate flavor.

Milk Chocolate
- Weston- Their finest milk chocolate manufactured with flavor-grade cocoa beans to create a mild chocolate flavor.
- Ultimate Classic- A premium milk chocolate with a rich, smooth, creamy taste.
- Meadowland- A robust milk chocolate manufactured with milk crumb to create a European style elegance.
- Beach- Their lightest milk chocolate manufactured with mild-flavor cocoa beans and a generous amount of milk to create a very mellow, delicate flavor.

- D-Milk- Their most popular milk chocolate. A rich, full-bodied milk chocolate with a pleasant caramelized flavor.
- Wisconsin- A sweeter milk chocolate with more chocolate characteristics.
- Jersey- Similar to Wisconsin, but made with a lower viscosity for thinner enrobing.
- Molding Milk- Their lowest viscosity milk chocolate created for easier hollow molding and very thin enrobing.
- Daisy- Similar to Wisconsin, but made with a lower viscosity for thinner enrobing, panning, and hand-dipping.
- Penn- A high quality, mild flavored milk chocolate.
- Meadowland II- A robust milk chocolate with dominant milk and chocolate characteristics.
- Rainier- One of their finest milk chocolates, using a blend of mild flavored cocoa beans to emphasize creamy milk notes.
- Milkmaid- A premium milk chocolate with a delicate balance of milk chocolate flavors.
- Whitney- A robust milk chocolate with rich, even chocolate characteristics.
- Western- Milk chocolate with a distinct chocolate flavor & milky notes.
- Golden- Similar to Western, but manufactured with a higher viscosity and finer particle size for a smoother texture.
- Lassen- Like the Golden, but refined even more to create a creamy, delicate flavor.

White Confectioner's Coating
- Corinthian- A high quality cocoa butter based "white chocolate" with smooth, creamy flavor.
- Mannitol White- Made with cocoa butter and sweetened with mannitol.

GHIRARDELLI
- Unsweetened Chocolate
- Bittersweet Chocolate
- Sweet Dark Chocolate
- Semi-Sweet Chocolate
- Milk Chocolate
- Classic White Confection

GUITTARD
Chocolate liquor
- Oban- Natural process. A blend of the finest cocoa beans available. Full, smooth chocolate flavor. The uniform size wafer form assures quick, even melting.

Bittersweet Chocolate Couverture
- Gourmet Bittersweet- A very rich, full flavored bittersweet chocolate with a low viscosity.
- Oro Bittersweet Ribbon- A distinctive bittersweet flavor that is great for ganaches. The ribbon form provides handling convenience and fast melt characteristics.

Dark Chocolate Semi-Sweet Couverture
- Darkote Chunk- Convenient chunks of mild flavored chocolate melt quickly for ganaches and enrobing applications.
- Lustrous- Robust chocolate flavor with a vanilla character. This is an all purpose chocolate that compliments any center.
- B/R Dark- A mild flavored chocolate that is a perfect accompaniment for delicate centers.
- French Vanilla- Guittard's blend of the finest flavor beans produces a chocolate with a rich, robust flavor and a distinct vanilla character.
- Molding Solitaire- A fine flavored, dutched, dark chocolate with a low viscosity for detailed molding applications.
- Solitaire- An enrobing viscosity similar in color and flavor to Molding Solitaire.
- Ramona- Their popular semi-sweet chocolate with a mild, well-rounded, dutched chocolate flavor.
- Monaco- Very mild and smooth. Perfect for ganaches and centers.

Milk Chocolate Couverture
- Old Dutch Milk- A standard of excellence with a medium strength chocolate flavor. The pleasing compliment for your enrobed centers.
- Grandeur- Smooth mild flavor with a well-blended, even chocolate profile.
- Belmont- Darkest of their milk chocolates with a full milk and full strength chocolate flavor yet with a mellow finish.
- Highland- Full chocolate flavor that is perfect for enrobed products. Especially good with nutmeats.
- Molding Heritage- Low viscosity chocolate designed for use with highly detailed molds. Medium strength chocolate with a pleasant milk flavor.
- Heritage- A medium viscosity chocolate similar in flavor to Molding Heritage. Great for enrobing.
- Signature- Silky smooth with a slight caramel flavor note. Medium strength chocolate and medium milk taste profile.

White Confectioner's Coating
- High Sierra- A cocoa butter white with a creamy flavor and smooth, buttery texture.
- White Satin- The premium white coating is flavored with cocoa butter and the essense of pure vanilla. Its silky-smooth mouth feel, delightfully lingering taste and superior meltability remind you of the highest quality chocolate.

HAWAIIN VINTAGE CHOCOLATES "Pistoles" (small disks)-48 pound cases

- '94Kea'au (Kilauea) 64% Couverture- Their Signature Couverture. A Hawaiian Vintage Chocolate original, their ´94 Kea'au Vintage is an exceptionally smooth chocolate with a strong, bordeaux-winy presence that possesses deep,earthy, lava tones and a multi-level lingering finish.
- '94 Hodge's-Single Estate (Kona) 64% Couverture-Hawaiian Vintage Chocolates is now producing a chocolate so rare it comes in Estate

Vintages. This chocolate has a nuttiness wrapped in buttery overtones of tropical fruit, and followed by a warm and sensual finish.

- Snows of Mauna Kea- Hawaiian White Chocolate- An unforgettable white with a 35% cocoa butter content and the caramel caresses of genuine Pacific vanilla.

MERCKINS

Chocolate Liquor

- Merckens Robin Liquor™- A blend of natural and Dutched liquors, with a rich, chocolate flavor.

Dark Chocolate Coatings

- Bordeaux BR™-Mellow,chocolate rich flavor notes with a reddish cast.
- Cabot BR™- A special blend enriched with chocolate crumb.
- Orleans BR™-Slightly lighter with a more mellow flavor than Bordeaux.
- Linwood™- A smooth bitter sweet chocolate with a vanilla background.
- Mansfield™- A slightly bittersweet chocolate with a vanilla background.
- Merit BR™- A mild, bittersweet chocolate flavor background.
- Princess™- A rich, bittersweet chocolate, which is Dutch processed.
- Richmond BR™- A fondant processing vanilla coating,slightly bitter, with a fruity flavor note.
- Tehuantepec™- A classical European fondant process chocolate coating.
- Yucatan BR™ Buttons- Their most popular vanilla flavored coating. Balanced chocolate flavor compliments all types of centers.
- Monopol™- Their darkest chocolate coatings, Dutched-processed, yet not overpowering in flavor.

Milk Chocolate Coatings

- Chautaugua™- Their lightest milk chocolate coating with a caramelized taste.
- Sharon™- A very light milk chocolate coating, enhanced by a light, golden color.
- Zurich™- A light milk chocolate coating with a delicate aromatic chocolate flavor.
- Zurich Buttons™- Their Zurich coating in a button form for ease of melting.
- Clover™- In between the color of Zurich and Marquis, this milk chocolate has a golden yellow hue.
- Gloria™- Similar in color and flavor to Marguis, but specially formulated with extra cocoa butter to promote ease in hollow molding.
- Gloria Buttons™- Their Gloria coating in button form for ease of melting.
- Luxurie™- A chocolate coating with a rich milk flavor.
- Marquis™- The crown jewel of their line as well as their most popular milk coating. Marquis has a rich dairy and chocolate flavor.
- Marquis Buttons™- Their Marquis coating in button form for ease of melting.

- Model™- Used for hollow molding. Same color and flavor as Marquis, thinned with lecithin.
- Golden Medallion™- A coating with a strong milk chocolate flavor.
- Epicure D™-A strong milk chocolate with a fruit note and milky flavor
- Montrose™- Balanced chocolate and milk flavor, ideal for almost any kind of center.
- Guernsey™- Robust chocolate flavor with a pleasant milky background note.
- Lorraine™- A rich chocolate flavor enhanced by chocolate crumb.
- Geneva™- Full bodied fondant process milk coating with a distinctive chocolate character.
- Mansfield™- A quality milk chocolate coating that can be used in a variety of applications.
- Performance™- Robust chocolate flavor with an underlying sweet milk character.

White Confectioner's Coating
- Ivory™- The original white coating with a cocoa butter base. Creamy color and taste balanced by a pleasing flavor.

NESTLÉS PETERS

Peter's® Chocolate Liquors
- Jewel- A full-roast, natural processed liquor. Their most popular liquor for general use.
- No. 23- A medium-roast, natural processed liquor which is especially treated to conform to stringent microbiological specifications.
- Broken Orinoco- A Dutch-processed liquor with a reddish hue and high coloring strength which is kibbled for ease of handling. A favorite for fudge making.

Peter's® Bittersweet Chocolate
- Gibralter- A true bittersweet chocolate specially adapted to blend with sweet centers. Excellent for chocolate-covered mints.

Peter's® Semi-sweet Chocolates
- Monogram- A full dark roast vanilla chocolate with fruity/smoky overtones. An excellent match with cordial cherries.
- Viking®- A full roast chocolate, used when a mild bittersweet flavor is desired. Preferred by bakers.
- Newport- Specially roasted levels of the beans provide a strong chocolate flavor.
- Zenda®- A well-rounded, slightly spicy chocolate flavor.
- Burgundy®- Their most popular semi-sweet chocolate. Has a reddish cast and a fruity, winy flavor note.
- Masterpiece®-Dutched chocolate with a flavorful hint of mild vanilla
- Commander®- A milder chocolate with a subtle nutty flavor. The rich brown color and flavor combine well in nut clusters.

Peter's Milk Chocolates
- Ultra®- Their lightest colored milk chocolate with a very distinct flavor resulting from unique flavor beans.
- Superfine- A golden-colored milk chocolate with spicy over tones.

- Orkney-A sweet milk chocolate with a caramel-like flavor background.
- Crema®-A typical Swiss styled milk chocolate with a medium strength chocolate flavor, popularly used with peanut-flavored centers.
- Broc®- Their most popular milk chocolate, the original Swiss formula has a predominant milk flavor and is less sweet.
- Madison®- A fine flavor balance of milk chocolate make this product a natural for chocolate covered pretzels.
- Glenmere- A sweet and somewhat darker milk chocolate designed for enrobing; it especially compliments nut confections.
- Chatham®- This product has the most intense chocolate flavor of all their milk chocolates.
- Cremello- Quite similar in flavor to Chatham.

White Confectioner's Coating
- Nestlé® Snowcap®- Cocoa butter based, this coating is more flavorful and less sweet than most other available white coatings and has a distinct chocolate flavor and aroma.

Nestlé® Sugar Free Coatings
- Milk Chocolate-Flavored-Made with Peter's Chocolate Liquor assuring consistent superior taste, it has a clean character with a delicate balance of chocolate and milk flavors. Excellent for use in sugar free chocolate truffle center or frosting.
- Dark Chocolate-Flavored- Dark Chocolate flavored sugar free coating is also made with Peter's Chocolate Liquor.It has a mild dark chocolate flavor with spicy overtones which is especially good in sugar free mint meltaways.
- White-The sugar free equivalent of Nestlé Snowcap.Ideal for sugar free white bakery and confectionery applications from mousse to white-coated pretzels.

VAN LEER

Dark and Bittersweet Chocolates
- New Amsterdam- A medium/dark colored chocolate recommended for enrobing and molding.
- Van Stever- A medium/dark colored chocolate recommended for enrobing and molding.
- Westport- A medium/dark colored chocolate recommended for molding.
- Nice- A medium/dark colored chocolate recommended for molding.
- Brielle- A medium/dark colored chocolate recommended for enrobing.
- 1121-115 Bittersweet- A very dark colored chocolate recommended for baking and making ganache.

Milk Chocolates
- Ardsley- A medium/light colored chocolate recommended for enrobing and molding.
- Delft- A medium colored chocolate recommended for enrobing and molding.

- Elburg- A very light colored chocolate recommended for enrobing and molding.
- Elburg Light- A very light colored chocolate recommended for enrobing and molding.
- Van Roos- A medium/dark colored chocolate recommended for enrobing and molding
- Utrecht- A medium/dark colored chocolate recommended for baking and molding.
- Rotterdam- A medium light colored chocolate recommended for enrobing and molding.
- Brussels- A medium/light colored chocolate recommended for enrobing and molding.
- Bergan- A medium colored chocolate recommended for enrobing and molding.
- Leerdam- A dark colored chocolate recommended for enrobing and molding.

White Confectioner's Coating
- Mendham White- A white colored confectioner's coating recommended for enrobing and molding.

WILBUR

Chocolate Liquor
- Reo Liquor- A fine, all-purpose natural process liquor.

Dark Chocolate Coatings
- Bronze Medal (BR) - Their most popular vanilla semi-sweet, with rich, smooth chocolate flavor. An ideal compliment to a variety of centers.
- Velvet (BR)- Their darkest vanilla semi-sweet with an intense chocolate character.
- S-272 Dark Sweet Chocolate- A basic dark sweet chocolate coating for general use.
- Empire- A dark, sweet chocolate with a subtle sweetness.
- Warwick (Parve)- A dark, sweet chocolate with a hint of bitterness to compliment sweet centers.
- Brandywine- A true bittersweet chocolate with deep color and minimal sweetness, Brandywine compliments a very sweet or highly flavored center. Also used for baking.

Milk Chocolate Coatings
- Cashmere- The smoothest of a well-balanced blend of fine milk chocolate flavor attributes. One of their very best.
- Sable- The same fine smoothness and balance of Cashmere in a milk chocolate with reduced viscosity.
- Medo-Gold- Their mild and creamy chocolate with a fresh milk note.
- Alpine- The same mild creaminess and fresh milk note as Medo-Gold with a reduced viscosity.
- Sunnybrook- Stronger chocolate character with a pleasant milky background.

- Cupid- Extensive conching gives a superb flavor profile of rich chocolate and creamy milk with a lightly caramelized character.
- Meadowbrook-Smooth, creamy, yet possessing a bold chocolate flavor
- Guernsey- A strong chocolate impact with a fresh milk undetone.
- Lancaster-A strong chocolate impact with a milk undertone.
- Cremolite- Their darkest milk chocolate with the strongest chocolate impact.
- D-408 Milk Chocolate Coating- A basic milk chocolate coating for general use.

White Confectioner's Coatings
- Ermine White Cocoa Butter Coating- Finest milk and cocoa butter are blended to create this true premium "White Chocolate" coating.
- Platinum White Cocoa Butter Coating- Made with deodorized cocoa butter, as well as regular cocoa butter and whole milk, Wilbur's Platinum coating offers a clean taste that leaves the mouth quickly, while a rich Bourbon vanilla adds to its unique European character. The faint, yet recognizable chocolate flavor is apparent to the most critical taste buds.

Imported "White" and Chocolate

CACAO BARRY-FRANCE
- Barry Grand Caraque- Pure Chocolate Liquor (unsweetened).
- Barry Concord Lenotre Bit-Sweet
- Barry Mi-Amere Semi-Sweet Couverture
- Barry Pure Milk Chocolate "Lacte"
- Barry Pure White Chocolate "Blanc"
- Barry Orange Chocolate Couverture- Semisweet orange flavor.
- Barry Glandujas Pure Chocolate with Hazelnut Flavoring

CALLEBAUT-BELGIUM
- Callebaut Pure Chocolate Liquor- with 54 percent cocoa butter fat.
- Callebaut Bittersweet Chocolate
- Callebaut Semi-Sweet Chocolate
- Callebaut Milk Chocolate
- Callebaut White Chocolate

CARMA-SWITZERLAND
All Carma Couvertures are perfect for truffle, praline and ganache production, flavoring of any creams, ice creams, parfaits, mousses and doughs, coating cakes or dipping cookies. Ideal for molding, decorating, and creating showpieces.

Chocolate Liquor
- Unsweetened Cocoa Block- Is compatible with all couvertures, so you may tailor the couvertures to your personal taste and degree of chocolate flavor you want to achieve.

Bittersweet Couverture
- Elite Bittersweet- Robust in flavor and deep brown in color. Ideal for ganaches or as a flavoring for any cream or filling.

Semisweet Couverture
- Bourbon Swiss Top Blocks
- Swiss Line Blocks
- Swiss Line Chocolate "Coins", dark- Are time and labor saving.

Milk Couverture
- Swiss Line Blocks

White Couverture
- Swiss Line Blocks- May be colored.
- Swiss Line Chocolate "Coins", white- Are time and labor saving.

LINDT-SWITZERLAND
- Lindt Courant- Bittersweet Chocolate.
- Lindt Excellence- Semi-sweet Chocolate.
- Lindt Surfin- Semi-sweet Chocolate.
- Lindt Milk- Milk Chocolate.
- Lindt Blancor- Cocoa Butter White.

VALRHONA-FRANCE
Chocolate Liquor
- Cocoa pate- Unsweetened chocolate.

Bittersweet Chocolate
- Maitre Chocolatier- A dark chocolate with a delicate fruity taste. Excellent for soft ganaches, diping and molding.
- Extra Bitter- An outstanding couverture with an intense bitter flavor and fragrance. Excellent for baking and for preparations requiring a flavor without a large quantity of chocolate.
- Manjuri (Grand Cru)-Long winey bittersweet flavor and incredible aroma. Excellent for mousses and ganaches.
- Pur Cariabe (Grand Cru)- A dark brown full but drier bittersweet taste. Excellent for mousses, ganaches, and molding.

Semi-sweet Chocolates
- Equatoriale- A brilliant warm colored chocolate that melts beautifully. Its light quality lends itself to fruit and liqueur flavorings.
- Caraque- A soft, full-bodied flavoring considering its high cocoa content. An excellent enrober for nut candies.
- Extra Noir- A true all-purpose semisweet chocolate that can be used in all confectionary applications.

Milk Chocolates
- Guanaja Lactee- The most exquisite of milk chocolates. Its wide range of uses includes enrobinng and elaborate prepartions.
- Jivara Lactee-A unique milk chocolate combining the flavors of brown sugar, malt, and vanilla with cocoa. Ideal for molding and dipping.

White Chocolate
- Ivoire- The finest white chocolate available. Made from Madagascar vanilla combined with high milk content and extremely pure cocoa butter.

Chapter

3

Getting
Started

Welcome To My Candy Room

Now that you are well versed in the differences that exist between chocolate coating, white confectioner's coating and compound coating, for the sake of simplicity I am going to refer to the three different types as "coating." Unless specifically specified, all the information that follows can be applied to whichever type of product you decide to use.

Your neighborhood candy supply store is the best place to start when you are going to purchase the ingredients needed for your first project. There you will find different types of chocolate and chocolate-like products. Most stores will let you sample different brands and even offer suggestions on which type will best suit your needs. Most stores deal with many different manufacturers, and are able to obtain a particular item upon request. They also sell many of their candy products in bags from one to ten pounds, so you do not have to purchase large amounts. If you do not have a store in your area, you can order products by phone from specialty shops and supply houses, and then have the products delivered to your home.

When you become more familiar with the techniques described in this book and are ready to make large pieces or large quantities, you may prefer to buy your ingredients in bulk. I purchase my compound coatings in the form of small circles, about the size of a nickel, in thirty-to-fifty pound boxes. When I use chocolate or white confectioner's coatings, I receive them in ten to thirteen pound blocks. Buying in bulk is less expensive than buying a pound at a time, but remember, you either use it or lose it; chocolate and chocolate-like products have a long shelf life, but they need to be stored properly because they will not keep indefinitely.

After you have purchased your coating, there is very little in the way of equipment and supplies that you will need for your first candy project. You probably have many things in your own kitchen; others can be purchased from a candy supply store, the kitchen sections of department stores, supermarkets or through mail-order. I started out on a wing and a prayer and now have "Mom's Candy Room." After a time (a very short time), my enthusiasm over powered my kitchen. I fell in love with and started collecting many of the different molds that were available. A frequent visitor to all the supply stores in my area, the owners got to know me so well, they would put things aside for me or call me at home when they had something unique.

There was a store that went out of business not far from my home; one of my chocolate suppliers bought the contents of the store. One day when I went to pick up chocolate, the owner came out and told me I could purchase boxes full of molds at a token of what they were worth. Talk about letting a kid loose in a candy store... Another store owner, Rosie, has what she calls the "archives." After being in business for over twenty-five years, she has an exorbitant number of molds that are not available anymore. Periodically, she will call me and let me rummage through some boxes. She knows I love characters from my children's shows and books; with her help, I have been able to acquire a treasure trove of childhood stars. I can not emphasize enough how important your supplier can be to your candy making.

As I was saying, I overstayed my welcome in the kitchen. You could say my cupboards runneth over. It was Christmas time, and we were molding the most spectacular Christmas tree. The mold belonged to a friend of mine, Fran Hurst, who had it for over thirty years. The details on the branches and the unique form of the tree made it the most requested piece. I complemented it by placing a candy train and track at the bottom with different colored presents piled all around.

A candy store that was filled with cookies was another big hit that year (when the snow covered roof was lifted off it was like an old fashioned candy dish). Fifteen trees and a dozen candy stores lined my counter top (you could not see the counter for the trees). Needless to say, it was the last year I made candy in the kitchen. My husband Stephen, the chef in our home, declared his kitchen off limits and I was banished to the storage room down stairs.

When we converted our basement into a play area for our five children, we left a storage room off to one side which is now my candy room. People ask me all the time how I manage to make so much candy with my children under foot. I have a gate in the doorway to keep our two year old twins restricted to their area, while allowing me to keep a watchful eye on them with visits and requests "piece peeese." The older kids (and even hubby) help me with some of the easier things when it gets real busy. If you do not have a room to call your own, claim a cupboard, pantry shelf or closet that you can store your supplies in.

Storing Your Coatings

Proper storage of coatings is very important. Coatings are vulnerable to foreign odors, so they must be wrapped and stored in air tight containers, in a room which is between 65-70 degrees F. with a relative humidity of 50 percent or lower. If the coatings are subjected to drastic differences in temperature, bloom will result (the fats in the coatings separate and whitish-gray spots or streaks appear on or throughout the coating's surface). This does not make the coatings unsuitable for use, just ugly in appearance. Once the coating is melted (or tempered if you are using white confectioner's coating or chocolate) the bloom will disappear. Never store coatings in the refrigerator. This will cause the coating to sweat when it is brought back to room temperature and moisture will develop on its surface. Moisture or water will alter the coating's appearance and also cause it to get thick and fudgie.

The shelf life among the different coatings and brands differ because of the variety of ingredients used. With proper storage, unsweetened chocolate has a shelf life of several years; dark chocolate lasts longer than two years; milk chocolate, one to two years, and white confectioner's coating and compound coatings, one year or less. I rarely, if ever, have coatings longer than six months. It's my personal preference. I have found that after a six-month period, the coatings do not melt and set up as easily as the new coatings do. I limit my coating use in the summer months and take extra care of any leftover coating. They store better if your home is air conditioned. When my candy making starts to pick up again (usually the end of September for Halloween), I buy new coatings and mix them with the leftovers, using a ratio of two parts new to one part leftover.

Melting

No matter which coating you are using, when melting never allow the temperature to rise above 120°F. You need to melt your coatings slowly and with caution. There is no remedy for scorched or burnt coating; when coatings scorch, they become grainy, stink, discolored, unusable, and have to be thrown out. Unsweetened chocolate will liquefy when it is melted, but all other types of coatings will hold their shape and appear not to have melted until they are stirred. Coatings will continue to melt even after being removed from the heat source.

Tempering Chocolate and White Confectioner's Coating

When using these cocoa butter-based coatings for dipping, enrobing, and molding candy, they must be in temper to avoid ugly bloom and poor set up (rehardening) of the coating.

There are several ways to temper coatings. I have chosen the ones I feel are the most widely accepted and least intimidating to master. Tempering does require patience and, at first, seems a bit challenging, but is well worth the effort. You will need to have *an accurate, easy-to-read thermometer with a range from 60 degrees F. to 120 degrees F.* There are people who have mastered the art of tempering and can gauge the temperature of coatings by feel, either with their hands or by touching the coating to their lip; but, believe me, when you are just starting out, you will need the thermometer.

I prefer to use my microwave for melting, as we go back a long way and have, by trial and error, come to know to the exact second how long it takes to melt the coatings. When using a microwave, the amount of time it takes to melt the coatings depends upon:

- The wattage of the oven
- The amount of coating being melted
- The size of the pieces of coating being melted
- The size of the container holding the coating
- The amount of cocoa butter present in the coating

My advice to you is: go slow. Heat the coating at a lower level of power (start with 30 percent) until you become familiar with how *your* oven behaves with coatings, then proceed to a higher power. If you are using a coating which comes in block form (instead of small discs), chop it up. Use either a food processor, a chef's knife or a hand grater to break the coating into small nickel to quarter size pieces. Do not use a blender—the coatings will cake in the bottom. Use an uncovered microwave safe container. I use a 1-quart clear glass Pyrex® measuring cup with a handle and pouring spout. A clear container enables you to see how the coating is melting. The coating will change from dull to shiny even though it may not look melted (remember, sweetened coatings hold their shape until stirred.) The spout is more convenient and less time consuming than using the spooning technique (Chapter 4, *Making Molded Magic).* The 1-quart size holds 1½ to 2 pounds of coating which is the most I melt at a time. More than two pounds gets a little crazy and less than 1½ pounds cools too fast. Do not cover the container you are melting coatings in. Moisture can develop on the cover and drop into your coating; this will cause the coating to get thick.

Microwave Method

1. Place your container of chopped coating in the microwave.
2. At 30 percent power, heat coating for 45 seconds.
3. Remove container and stir the coating, which should be partially melted.
4. Check the temperature with the thermometer, your goal is 110°-120° F.
5. If the coating has not reached the desired temperature, return the container to the microwave and heat at 10 to 20 second intervals, removing, stirring, taking its temperature each time.
6. When the coating is 110°-120° F., remove it from the oven, pour 2/3 of it onto a marble slab or equivalent flat surface (glass, Formica, poly, stainless-steel, Corian®, but no wood, as it holds moisture, odors and can splinter).
7. Using an offset spatula, spread the coating out over the slab.
8. Using a pastry scraper, gather the coating into a pool in the center of the slab and take a temperature reading. (The object is to bring the temperature of the coating down to 80° F., so steps seven and eight may have to be repeated several times.)
9. When the temperature of the coating is 80° F., using the pastry scraper, scrape the coating back into the original container with the other third coating. Mix thoroughly. You are trying to achieve a temperature of 86°-90° F. for dark chocolate and 84°-88° F. for milk chocolate and white confectioner's coating. When you have reached this temperature, your coating is in good temper.
10. Mold or dip your candies but maintain the temperature of your coating by placing the container on a heating pad or warming tray.

Double Boiler Method

1. Fill the bottom pan of a double boiler with enough water to just touch the bottom and sides of the top pan when it is inserted.
2. Put the chopped coating into the top pan. Do not cover or get any water in the pan containing the coating.
3. Place the double boiler on the stove and heat slowly so no boiling water or steam splatters into the top pan. Stir occasionally and take its temperature.
4. When the temperature of the coating has reached 110°-120° F., remove the top pan from the double boiler.
5. Carefully wipe the bottom of the pan so you do not accidently get any drops of water in your coating.
6. Continue following steps 6 through 10 of the microwave method.

Alternative Method

An electronic tempering machine is a great alternative to hand tempering. There are several companies that manufacture them for the small store owner or enthusiastic home candy maker, but they are costly. One machine that is new to the market is manufactured specifically for the home candy maker and is reasonably priced. Unfortunately, there was not enough time to acquire this machine and test it out before the publication of this book; but I was impressed with the literature I read on it, so I thought it was worth mentioning to you. It is called the *Sinsation™ Chocolate Maker,* and is made by *Chandré.* The address is in the reference section along with other tempering machine manufacturers.

Melting Compound Coatings

My first candy making attempt was with compound coating. I went to a supply store near my home called Chocolate Treats and More. The owner, Amelia Murphy, was very understanding and receptive to my needs. I came to her with no knowledge of candy making whatsoever, only a strong desire to make beautifully molded candies. She gave me a tour of her store and working area, showing me all the candies she had made, supplies she used, explaining how to use them as she went along. I left her store armed with two pounds of Merckens' Pastel Coatings (one pound each of Rainbow White and Rainbow Orange), a bag of lollipop sticks, a bag of poly bags, and two molds. One was a pumpkin and the other a ghost (It was September and I wanted to try making Halloween pops). When I arrived home to start my project, I realized I did not have a double boiler. Improvise! I took a Pyrex® bowl out of the cupboard, placed it on top of a small pot filled with water, nearly touching the Pyrex®. I turned on the stove and presto, melted my coating. My first experiment was a success. Even though making lollipops with compound coating is probably one of the easiest things to accomplish, it gave me the encouragement to advance to more difficult things.

Melting compound coating is a simple procedure. As with cocoa butter-based coating, the temperature of the coating should never rise above 120° F. No steam, water, or moisture should ever come in contact with your coating. If you are using coating in block form, chop it into small pieces. I usually melt only two pounds at a time.

Double Boiler Method

1. Place just enough water into the bottom portion of the double boiler so it does not come in contact with the top portion when it is inserted.
2. Placing only the bottom portion on the stove, heat the water to near boiling and then remove it from the stove.
3. Place your chopped coating in the top portion and insert it into the bottom portion carefully.
4. Let the heat generated from the water start to melt your coating, and then give it an occasional stir. Do not beat or whip the coating, this will cause air bubbles to form.
5. When the coating is completely melted and has a smooth consistency (no lumps) your coating is ready to use.

Microwave Method

1. Place chopped coating into a microwave-safe container.
2. Using 30 percent power, heat coating for one minute, then stir.
3. Continue to heat and stir coating at 20 second intervals until it is completely melted and has a smooth lump free consistency.
4. Your coating is now ready to use.

Chapter

4

Making Molded
Magic

Molding Your Imagination

What separates a good piece of candy (are there really any bad ones?) from a spectacular piece of candy is simply... imagination. Molding by definition is using a pattern or form to give shape to another thing. Children use their imaginations to create the most wonderful things: the refrigerator box becomes a castle or space ship; inner tubing from paper towels becomes the evil magician's wand. In this chapter I will explain the use of the popular types of molds and illustrate ways to unlock your imagination to mold and create your own unique and magical candies.

Golden Oldies

When candy makers first started molding their coatings, the molds they used were made from metal. They were sturdy and lasted a long time. You can still find these types of molds, not just at Grandma's house or in antique stores; some companies still manufacture these replicas of old. They are more expensive than the modern plastic type and the variety is limited. For the history buff, there is a book, *Chocolate Moulds: A History & Encyclopedia, by Judene Divone (Oakton Hills Publications)* which is an illustrated book of molds from the 1800s to the 1970s. If you are ever near Lititz, Pennsylvania, you can visit the *Candy Americana Museum & Store* of The Wilbur Chocolate Company. For information, call (717)626-3249.

Plastic Candy Molds

Today, the most common molds for coatings are the less expensive ones made from an FDA approved high-grade clear plastic, which come in an infinite variety of sizes and shapes. Some companies offer different grades of plastic molds. There is a very hard plastic designed primarily for the commercial trade, and a thinner more pliable plastic designed for the hobbyist. If you find yourself working with a large mold that requires several pounds of coating, you may find it easier to use the heavier commercial type of mold.

I once had an order for 150 lollipops of a special bear for a child's birthday party. Each bear had to be hand painted in two different colors, and then poured in milk chocolate. I had one mold which contained three individual bears. You guessed it; I painted that mold 50 times. It was a very time consuming order which would have been a snap if I had had several molds. In my defense, it was an old mold which was not available anymore and I was one of the lucky few who had it. For the popular characters that come out now however, I make it a point to purchase at least two.

Flat Molds

A flat mold is a sheet of plastic containing one or more different cavities, which can be either all the same shape, or a variety of shapes and sizes. Most of your lollipop molds are flat molds that are very easy with which to work. The lollipop molds have indentations for you to place a stick. Your molded candies, then, will have a dimensional front and a flat back.

3-Dimensional Molds

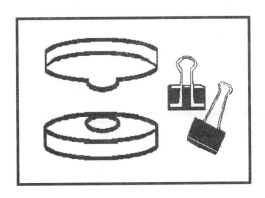

3-dimensional molds are two or more mold pieces that are joined together to form a 3-dimensional candy. There are small projections on one side of the mold which fit nicely into the hollows on the other side. This ensures that the two pieces line up correctly. Clips are used to secure the two pieces together. I like to use binder clips to secure my 3-D molds. They come in several sizes and can be bought at office supply stores. I also trim the excess plastic from the mold which makes it easier to get a tight seal around the mold (creating less trim work).

3-D molds can be either open or closed ended; closed ended molds have to be filled prior to joining the pieces together; open ended molds are filled after they are joined together.

BEFORE YOU BEGIN MOLDING

Your chocolate or white confectioner's coating should be in a good tempered state, or if you are using a compound coating, it should be melted to a smooth consistency. The molds you are using should be in front of you. All required materials should be on hand, i.e., lollipop sticks, clips for 3-D molds, etc.

Using a Flat Mold

There are several methods you can use to get the coating into the mold; I will list all of them and you can decide which one you prefer.

Spooning the coating into the mold is probably the safest and easiest way for a beginner. I prefer to use an icetea spoon. It has a long handle and a small bowl which makes pouring into small cavities easier.

Another way to fill a mold is by using a container with a pouring spout. You can gently pour the coating into the mold. This method does take practice, though, to avoid over-filling the mold.

Yet another way to fill a mold is by using a decorating bag and piping the coating in the mold. This method is convenient for making very small decorative pieces. This method requires some practice to gain control of the flow of the coating. You can use either a reusable bag or the new convenient disposable ones. Just fill the bag, leaving enough room at the top to hold it, and snip the point off the bottom to let the coating out. If you would rather make one yourself from waxed or parchment paper, follow the directions below:

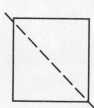

1. Cut paper into a 12-inch square. Cut each square in half to form two triangles

2. Roll each triangle into a cone by wraping the two outer points, one around the other, towards the center.

3. Fold down the points to hold it securely.

Do not get upset if you over fill a mold. When the coating sets, the edges can be trimmed and no one will ever know. Some people purposely over fill and glide a metal scraper across the mold to remove the excess coating before cooling it. I try to come just up to the edge of the cavity purposely under filling it a bit. If you are making 100 lollipops, not having to trim them is a great time saver. After you have filled all the cavities on your mold, tap the entire mold on the counter a couple of times to even out the coating and release any air bubbles that may have gotten caught in the mold. If you raise the mold and look at the underside, you will see if there are any bubbles. Take note of how shiny the coating looks at this point; when the coating sets (hardens), the mold will have a frosted appearance.

If you are making a lollipop, insert the stick into the indentation provided and give the stick a little turn. This will ensure that the coating covers the stick (giving it a nicer appearance), and will also give it a better hold on the finished pop. Put the mold on a level surface in the refrigerator to set. After you become more familiar with molding you can advance to the freezer. Putting the coating in the freezer takes less time, but you must be careful not to set the coating too quickly or it will crack.

After a few minutes, take the mold out of the refrigerator and hold it above your eye to look at the underside. You will notice that the coating has a frosty appearance. This means that it is ready to come out. If there are still shiny areas, put the mold back in the refrigerator and let it continue to set. If you attempt to unmold a piece that has not completely set, the coating will stick to the mold. If all areas are frosty, the piece is ready to come out. Gently turn the mold upside down over the counter and either give the mold a little twist, or tap it gently on the counter; your new molded pieces should pop right out. Now check the edges of your pieces. If there is an area that needs to be trimmed, first attempt to gently snap the extra off; if this does not work, get a very sharp paring knife and gently trim the edge.

Adding Color

Coatings can be purchased in a variety of colors: we can make green or brown leaves, and pour Easter eggs using beautiful pastel colors. Sometimes a splash of color added to a piece can change it from ordinary to extraordinary. I love to add color to my molded pieces. I do not consider myself an artist by any means (I can't draw a straight line without a ruler), but something magical happens when I sit at my counter and start coloring a piece. There is nothing more gratifying than seeing a child's smile when given a lollipop of his favorite character that actually looks just like it should. A molded house takes on a special charm when the details are in color. People will marvel at the detail and appreciate the extra effort put into a piece that is so realistic that they are not sure if they should eat it. Coloring is really easy and a lot of fun.

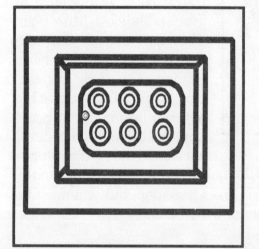

I have an old fashioned warming tray that I use. I set a clear rectangular Pyrex® dish on top of it, filled ⅓ of the way with water. I put little Pyrex® custard dishes, each filled with a different color coating, inside the larger dish, making sure no water gets inside the coatings. You can use a variety of household items to accomplish the same thing. If you have an electric skillet, you can fill it with water and put custard dishes or small glass cups inside, keeping the temperature on a low setting. Another method is to use a cupcake tin inserted in a warming tray. If you use this method, you can use disposable cupcake liners for an easier clean-up. *The Wilton Company* also makes the *Wilton Candy Melting Plate*, a microwavable palette that holds up to eleven different colors.

For the sake of convenience, you may want to purchase different colored compound coatings. Remember, many compound coatings are not compatible with the cocoa-butter in white confectioner's coating and chocolate. If you are planning to add color to a cocoa-butter based coating, you will have to add color to a white confectioner's coating or a compound coating made with a non-lauric fat. Coloring your own coatings gives you a wider variety of colors from which to choose.

To create your own colors, melt your coating according to the specified type, and then add coloring. You can not use regular food coloring in your coatings! These contain water which will stiffen your coating. Use, instead, a coloring paste or powder. The coloring I prefer is *Candy Color by Chefmaster®*. It is a vegetable-based coloring made specifically for coatings. Two other colorings are: *Paste Food Coloring by Country Kitchen* and *Spectrum Paste Food Coloring by Ateco*. They are available in candy supply stores.

Tips...Tricks... and Interesting Stuff

If you are using compound coatings and your colors seem a little thick, you may want to thin them out a bit. Add about a teaspoon of old-fashioned vegetable shortening. You can also use paramount crystals or lecithin, both available at candy supply stores.

Tips...Tricks... and Interesting Stuff

Painting

Paint the areas of your mold to which you want to add color before you pour your coating. This ensures a finished piece that is all even and shiny. If you apply color on a finished piece the coating is raised on the surface. This may be okay for eyes and other small details that you want raised, but for the overall affect, it is better to paint before you pour.

To apply color, I use the wrong end of a paintbrush. When first experimenting with coloring, I bought paintbrushes and literally painted in the color. This method was short lived for two reasons; first, periodically a bristle would break off into my coating and I would not realize this until the piece was finished. I would have to discard it and start over. Second, I just never could acquire the control over the brush, and would smear coating into areas that were not supposed to be colored. But turning the brush over and using the rounded end, I can dip it into the color and have better control over where the color goes. Brushes and handles come in different sizes. You can also use lollipop sticks to paint your molds and then discard them when you are through. Using a toothpick or a large hat pin for small details makes the job a snap.

When painting, everything is done in layers. For example, if you want to add color to a Santa face mold, you need to color the pupil of his eye first (a black dot); when that is dry (each layer must be thoroughly dry to prevent the colors from running), you would continue to the iris (a nice shade of blue); next you would give him rosy cheeks by applying a circle of pink to each one.

Multi-layered and Flavored candies

You can add a lot of pizazz to a simple bite-sized square of candy. Adding colors in layers, and/or flavoring the coating, making a bite-sized surprise.

To make layered candy, simply fill the cavity of your mold with your first color, ½ the way up for two colored candies, or ⅓ of the way up for three colored. Refrigerate until set. Now add the second color on top of this one and refrigerate again. Continue this method until you have added the desired number of layers.

You can either purchase flavored coatings (refer to the chapter *So Many Choices*) or add flavoring of your own to coatings. If you are going to add flavorings, always use oil flavorings; the alcohol and water in extracts will stiffen your coating. Flavorings are very concentrated, so use only a couple of drops at a time, and thoroughly mix the coating.

3-Dimensional Molded Candies

Most 3-dimensional molds do not lay flat on the refrigerator shelf. Before you begin, have something that you know will prop up your mold. Some things you might try are a drain board for dishes, or a slotted cake rack. For small molds a wide mouthed cup or jar can do the trick.

Solid Piece

If you are using an open ended mold, you clip it together and fill it; however, if you are using a closed ended mold, you have two options available when a solid piece is desired.

Method One

STEP: 1  STEP: 2  STEP: 3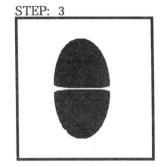

1. Fill one-half of the mold almost to the rim (about an ⅛ of an inch from the rim). Fill the other half of the mold all the way to the rim. Refrigerate both halves until set.
2. Take the two halves out of the refrigerator but do not remove the coating from the mold. Take some of your melted coating and top off the half that you did not fill all the way.
3. Gently place the other mold on top of it and clip them together. You must work fast because the cold from the molded piece will begin to set the added coating. Wait a few minutes, remove the clips and take your solid piece of candy out of the mold.

Method Two

This method is very easy, but understand that when you alter the mold, it is permanent. With a scissor or sharp knife, carefully cut an opening in the bottom of each half of the mold (creating an open ended mold). Clip the pieces together and fill the mold with melted coating. Refrigerate until set.

Semi-Solid or Hollow Candies

Method One

Using a closed ended mold, fill one half of the mold with melted coating. Clip the other half securely to it. Next rotate the mold in your hands, turning it until you see that all areas are covered. Put the mold in the refrigerator to chill. You must take it out and rotate it every couple of minutes to ensure that the coating is evenly distributed. After the coating has completely set, remove the mold. You now have a piece of candy that is hollow inside. You can also use this technique with an opened ended mold.

Method Two

Fill each side of the mold but do not clip together. Put them both in the refrigerator. After a couple of minutes, remove them (there should still be liquid in the center), invert them over a clean tray and let the liquid coating run out. There should be a thin shell of hardened coating remaining in the mold. If you want a thicker shell, add more coating to the mold and repeat the procedure. When you have the desired thickness, refrigerate until the coating has completely set. Now you have two hollow pieces. You can join them together by dabbing a small amount of coating on the rim of one side and then placing the other side on it.

Before you put them together, it is fun to add a small surprise inside. Place a trinket, jelly bean, bite-size piece of candy, etc. in one half before you close it.

Hunting For Molds

Using a store bought mold is not the only way to make molded candies. With a little imagination you can find an enormous number of containers that you can use as molds right in your house.

Let's start in the kitchen; open a cabinet and peek inside. Forget the clutter or mess; we're going on a mold hunt (not to be confused with the refrigerator kind)! Looking around, you'll probably come across a gelatin mold you always meant to use but never did. The bottom can be filled about a quarter-inch deep and refrigerated, and you will have a beautiful molded piece to place on top of a cake.

I'll bet you have a sheet cake pan and some old cookie cutters lying around too. If you pour coating into the sheet pan about a quarter-inch deep and refrigerate to set, but not harden all the way, you can take the cookie cutters and the shapes can be pressed into the coating. After pressing all the shapes, put the pan back into the refrigerator to set completely.

You can also place perimeter cookie cutters (the kind that have the outline of a shape with no top or bottom) on a sheet pan, fill them with coating and let set. Your pan must have a level surface—do not use the ones you let your kids beat on with the wooden spoons, or the coating will ooze out of the bottom of the cutters. You can also use a cookie cutter with a closed top, invert it over a cup so the handle is inside the cup, and the cutter lays flat. Pour coating in the cutter and let set.

Character pans make the most interesting recepticles for coatings. You can pour the coating right into the pan and let it set. The small individual child mini pans come in so many shapes and sizes, you are limited only by your imagination.

A friend had asked me to make favors for an "over the hill" party for her Dad's 65th birthday. She did not want anything too morose, like headstones or coffins, but something, none the less to poke fun at his age. We decided on a cane. Looking through my molds, all my canes were candy canes, the kind that had definate markings on them to indicate that they were Christmas candy canes. What to do…I found a plastic candy cane shaped container in a party store, the kind that you fill with trinkets or jelly beans. I decided to try it. Wanting the canes to be solid, I cut the bottoms of the containers off with a sharp knife. Since there were no edges to clip together, I held the two halves securely with a rubber band. They were filled with a dark bittersweet coating (the color was almost black) and put in the freezer to set. They came out great! They were wrapped in individual polyurethane bags and tied with a black ribbon imprinted "You're Over The Hill." They were a smash hit.

You can use any non-toxic container that is safe for use with food. The possibilities are endless. I have used every conceivable dish, bowl and pan in my kitchen and have even used some of my kids toys. Remember, any scratch or dent will be mirrored in your piece, and the container should be thoroughly cleaned and dried before use. Happy hunting!

Caring For Molds

Proper care of your molds will guarantee many satisfied years of use. The maintenance is minimal. You do not have to wash your molds every time you use them, but you must store them clean. When a holiday comes around, the molds that I am using for that season are brought out and hung on a peg board above my work table. I do not wash them until the season is over except if they are getting a bit chocolaty. I keep a very tidy work area, make a mess and straighten it up at the same time. Not that I'm a fanatic or anything; it's just less time consuming to be organized. If you get in the habit of putting something back where it belongs after you have used it, you will not have to spend time looking for it when you need it again. Coating can be messy...if you have a spill, cleaning the coating off a clean counter is much easier than washing everything that was in its path. I wash my molds in warm water and use *Dawn* liquid detergent. I experimented with a lot of different dish soaps before sticking with *Dawn*. You only need a few drops and it really cuts the greasy residue left on the mold. A quick drying with a soft cloth and you're done.

Tips...Tricks... and Interesting Stuff

Old-fashioned cotton diapers are great to use. They are soft, do not scratch the surface of the mold (a scratch will show up on your finished product) & are very absorbent.

Tips...Tricks... and Interesting Stuff

Large rubber storage chests make the greatest storage containers for molds. At least a dozen are stacked on top of each other in my candy room. The flat molds stack nicely in the 18-gallon size. They keep the molds dust free and in an upright position so they do not warp; they can be labelled so you know what's inside. My large 3-D molds are kept in clear zippered plastic bags (the kind blankets and sheets come in) and are hung from hooks on the ceiling.

Chapter

5

The Glory
of
Garnishing

To Garnish or Not To Garnish

That is the question...in my case there was no question. I was, and still am, a horrendous cook. I can bake and make candy, but when it comes to making the main course, if it isn't dessert...God help us all.

Growing up, everyone cooked in our house but me. My father, sisters and brother can cook, and my mother is an outstanding cook. Part of my father's job description was to frequently entertain his business associates (I think his boss loved mom's cooking, too). My dad could call my mother at noon and tell her he was bringing home a dozen guests for dinner at seven and she would whip up a dinner party without batting an eye. I mean, from soup to nuts, and then some. We had dinner guests so often we had dinner wear for twenty-four.

My options then were to either marry someone who was accomplished in the kitchen, or face a wrongful death suit from killing someone with my own cooking. I really can't explain my misfortune in the kitchen. As a child, I must have been too busy eating and enjoying all the wonderful things being prepared instead of paying attention to how they were prepared; since I never quite grasped the concept of cooking, I, instead, learned to garnish.

Adding a garnish to a dessert is a lot more fun than trying to masquerade your meatloaf. A simple garnish can change an ordinary dessert into an extraordinary dessert. If you are like me, when you bring a dessert to someone's home, you want to bring one that is tried and true. You can bring the same thing over and over again...just garnish it differently each time! The following pages are filled with wonderful garnishes that have enhanced my desserts and caused people to actually doubt that I can not cook. Now that is quite an accomplishment!

Tips...Tricks... and Interesting Stuff

When you are making garnishes, always remember to make more than you need. If one or two break, which usually happens, you will have extras on hand. If you get lucky and none break, you can always find a use for the extras, or melt them down again.

Tips...Tricks... and Interesting Stuff

Ruffles and Curls

Ruffles and curls are so delicate and feminine, they remind me of a time when little girls wore fancy dresses adorned with ruffles and bows over crinoline slips. This fragile looking garnish transforms a plain iced cake into a romantic and beautiful one. Ruffles are a little harder to master than curls, but even your less than perfect first attempts will make for a fantastic garnish.

Basic Instructions

You will need a flat cookie sheet or similar pan, a metal scraper or spatula, and melted coating. Using the metal scraper, spread your melted coating across the pan in a thin layer. Put the pan in the refrigerator to chill. Do not let the coating completely set. This is where you learn that patience is a virtue and practice is an understatement. Do not get discouraged if your coating gets too hard to curl the first few times; this is one of those trial and error things where there are too many variables to be able to give you an exact amount of time for chilling (how much coating you used, how thin the layer is, how cold your fridge is, etc.). However, you can guess that it is ready to curl when there is a dull look to the coating and you leave an indent in it when you press your finger on it. Coating which has hardened can be remelted and used again.

Ruffles

After following the basic instructions, take the metal scraper and, 1. starting at the edge of the pan, scrape the coating in a semi-circular motion. 2. Keeping the inside corner edge of the scraper in place, 3. move the outer edge in a semi-circle. The pieces of coating will ruffle and be fan like. Gently pick up the ruffle and place it aside. Your ruffles will not be exactly the same. However, if you like, each unique piece can be trimmed with a sharp knife before they completely harden.

Large Curls

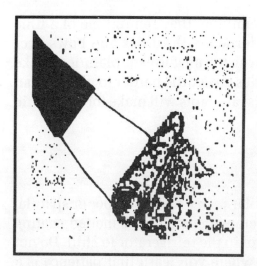

Large Curls (which we used to call chocolate cigarettes before it became politically incorrect) are pretty easy to make. Following the basic instructions, anchor your pan against your body and hold securely with one hand. Starting at the end close to your body, take the metal scraper and push it into the coating at an angle close to but not parallel to its surface. Scrape away from your body. Take the curls and place on a clean cookie sheet and refrigerate until completely hard.

You can make as many curls as you like. Stored in an air tight container, they can be kept refrigerated until you need them. I like to use a hard rubber container and gently place them in between layers of waxed paper. Remember, they are fragile, so place them somewhere where they will not be tossed around by hungry kids searching for the answer to "what's there to eat Mom?" or eaten by the kids thinking the curls were the answer.

Wedges and Cut Outs

Adding wedges or cut outs of candy around the sides of a cake can make an interesting effect with very little effort. Pour coating into a cookie sheet, spreading evenly and refrigerate, until it is almost set. With a sharp knife, cut into the coating the desired shapes. Refrigerate until completely set. Arrange the shapes around the edge of the cake. You can take a cookie cutter and press it into the coating to make special characters and shapes. Do not twist the cutter as you press. Push it in the coating firmly and pull it out in a straight upward motion.

Leaves

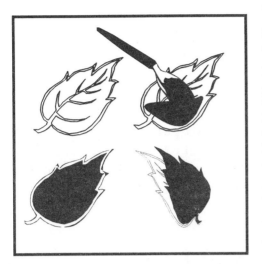

When a dessert calls for just a little something extra, candy leaves are just what you need. You can use a ready made mold to make them or you can make a more realistic leaf using a real leaf as the mold. Do not use just any leaf. Many plants are poisonous, make sure the one you use is non-toxic. Next, choose a leaf that has well defined veins and is large enough to be held by an edge. You may want to try rose, mint, grape, or lemon. Gently wash your leaves and dry thoroughly. Take a spoon or large paint brush and cover the bottom side of the leaves with coating, making sure not to overlap the edges (it will make it difficult to peel). Place the leaves coating-side-up to set. When the coating has set, gently peel the leaf from the coating. Presto!

Piping Coating

The leaf doesn't have to fall far from the tree for you to know how to make one. Branches and twigs are snaps to make when using a piping bag. As a matter of fact, there are many wonderful garnishes that are made by this

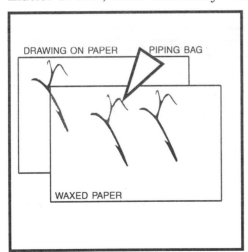

DRAWING ON PAPER   PIPING BAG

WAXED PAPER

technique. In chapter 4, *Making Molded Magic*, I demonstrated the use of a decorating bag in "Using a Flat Mold." The procedure for twigs and branches is basically the same. Draw branches or twigs on a piece of paper. Place them under a piece of waxed paper and pipe your coating over the outline of the design. Refrigerate until set. You must snip the end of the bag prior to filling it with coating. Control of the fluid coating is the thing you must master. The opening should be very small, just large enough so the coating will flow out with very little pressure applied to the bag. This will take some practice. Do not be surprised if the coating continues to flow out even after you stop applying pressure. To prevent this, just tilt the opening upwards. If the coating cools and hardens at the opening, you can make it fluid again by laying it on a warming tray or by pinching the end between your fingers and pushing the hardened coating out of the hole.

To familiarize yourself with using and gain control of the bag, the best thing to do, is to practice. Take a piece of waxed paper and put it on the counter. Practice piping (writing with the bag) your ABC's. You remember, when you were in third grade and had to write in cursive, *aaaabbbbcccc*. You can even involve your little ones at this point, every letter your little ones get correct, they get to eat. What a treat!

Filigree, Scroll Work and Lace

Some of the most beautiful designs are produced in filigree, scroll work and lace. Border a cake in a piece of chocolate lace and you can already hear the applause. A simple cup of ice cream becomes a spectacular dish when you add a filigree piece of candy peaking out of the top. And who could resist a dessert topped with an elegant piece of scrolled candy?

Tips...Tricks... and Interesting Stuff

Garnishes are very delicate and can melt quickly in your hand. To help prevent your pieces from melting, run your hands under cold water and dry them thoroughly before picking up your piece. You can also insert a toothpick in the space between two lines to carefully transfer a finished piece to its desired spot on your dessert.

Tips...Tricks... and Interesting Stuff

With a little patience and a steady hand, you can re-produce the delicate and intricate details in chocolate coating. All you need is a copy of a design. Transfer your design onto a piece of paper and cover it with waxed paper. Pipe the coating over the outline and let harden. Peel the waxed paper off and you have a showstopping piece of candy. You can copy patterns from real lace or photocopy different scrolls from magazines. You can also create designs with the aid of a computer and make copies in different sizes.

Candy Cones

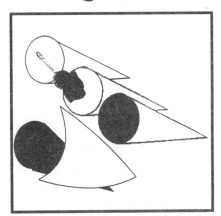

Candy cones are so versatile. You can simply arrange them in a circular fashion on the top of a cake or sprinkle them with cocoa powder or confectioner's sugar. For an added pleasure the cones can be filled with berries or pieces of fruit or even whipped cream. They also make slicing the cake easy, just cut in between the cones and everybody gets one!

Make a paper cone following the directions in chapter 4, *Making Molded Magic*. Instead of folding down the flaps, cut them off and secure the cone with a piece of tape on the outside. Make sure the entire inside of the cone is coated; you can do this by pouring a small amount of coating in the cone and use the back of a small spoon to spread it up the sides. Place the cones on a tray and refrigerate them. Do not let them stay too long in the fridge; cones can crack easily if chilled too long. Take the point of a sharp knife and slice the tape to free the paper; it will now peel off easily.

Silhouettes

Silhouettes, or shadows, as my son likes to call them, are very easy indeed. Take a picture of anything and place it under waxed paper. Pipe the outline of the picture and then fill it in with coating by piping in a back and forth motion or spooning a small amount of coating in the center of the picture and spreading it out towards the piped edges with a butter knife or the

bottom side of the spoon bowl. Refrigerate to set and then peel gently from waxed paper.

My children's coloring books make the greatest templates for this technique. The pictures are large and the outlines are thick and dark so I do not have to darken them. Your child can always have his or her favorite character made out of candy with this technique. You can add an individual candy to every child's cupcake to complement the theme of your party. This is a win-win situation, mom's the hero who made great candy; everybody gets to eat it; and somebody gets a new coloring book.

Brussels Sprout Roses

Nothing compares to the cheesecake my girlfriend Annie Kozak makes; it was love at first bite and I've never made a cheesecake since. She makes one for me for every occasion (God love her!) and I eat it everyday for breakfast and lunch until every delicious morsel is gone. Annie's cheesecake can not be improved, (it's that good) therefore, if she ever was inclined to do something different, garnishing it with brussels sprout roses would be the only thing to do.

Brussels sprout roses are made the same way chocolate leaves are made. Take a few uncooked brussel sprouts and cut the bottoms off. Remove the

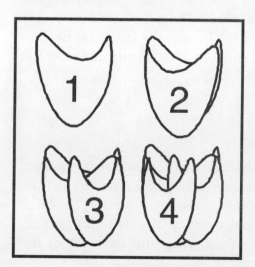

outer, firmer, layers and gently wash and thouroughly dry them. Brush the inside of each leaf with coating, making sure not to go over the edges or it will be hard to peel and refrigerate to set. After the coating has set, gently peel the leaf from your coating. Assemble the roses by placing a dab of coating on a piece of waxed paper and position two "petals" facing each other. Add petals around the coating in a shingle affect until you have achieved your desired look.

Chapter

6

Let's Take

a

Dip

Let's Get Busy!

For me, when it comes to dipping centers with coating, *I Love Lucy* always comes to mind. My favorite episode was the one when Lucy and Ethel took jobs in a candy factory on the assembly line. If you are not familiar with it, a brief description would be utter chaos. They were supposed to take candies and wrap them as they came down the conveyor belt. Needless to say, they could not keep up and started to stuff the candies in their mouths, in their pockets, etc.; it was a rip roaring sight…*classic Lucy*.

To avoid such chaos, organization and rhythm are the keys to successful candy dipping. Before you begin, arrange your work area and have a set game plan.

Making dipped candies is deceptively easy. Before you begin, make sure you have the following:

1. Melted compound coating, or tempered chocolate, or white confectioner's coating.
2. The food to be dipped.
3. Two cookie sheets lined with waxed paper.
4. A dipping fork or similar utensil.

Place your melted/tempered coating between your two cookie sheets. Have all your pieces to be dipped on one sheet and start dipping. It really is that easy. You just get into a nice, easy rhythm of picking up a piece, dipping it into the coating, and placing it on the other cookie sheet. You need to work quickly before your coating gets cold and starts to set. As you take the dipped candy from the bowl, gently touch it to the rim of your container to remove excess coating.

Dipped Fruit

Almost any fruit can be used for dipping, fresh or dried, but some require additional preparation.

1. All fruit should be washed and thoroughly dried.
2. Whole strawberries and cherries are easily handled if you keep the stem on and hold it to dip with.
3. Large or whole fruit like bananas or apples should have a lollipop stick or popsicle stick inserted before dipping.

4. Sliced fruit that can turn brown, like banana or apple should first be dipped into lemon juice or other acidic juice which prevents discoloration.
5. Small fruits like grapes or berries can be dipped using a toothpick or spooned into clusters.

Dipped fruit in and of itself is a wonderful treat. Who could resist a tray of succulent strawberries dipped in bittersweet chocolate? With a little imagination, you'll need to have extra on hand! To add a little pizazz to dipped strawberries, try dipping them first into white coating, three quarters of the way up to the stem. After the coating has set, redip the strawberry half the way up in white coating tinted blue. This makes a very patriotic display for fourth of July parties.

Crazy About Clusters

Candy clusters are the easiest candies to make. Any shape, any form, any kind. After you have been making candy for a while, you can pretty much gauge how much coating you will use, and have very little, if anything, leftover. This is good, but can be very disappointing to your children. I like to make clusters with any leftover melted coating. A small amount of nuts, raisins, cereal or coconut makes cleanup quick, easy, and keeps everybody happy. I just pour whatever I have in the cupboard right into my Pyrex® cup a little at a time, and stir until every piece is coated; then drop them by the tablespoon-full onto a waxed piece of paper to set.

Pretzels

How you dip pretzels depends on what size and style (stick or Bavarian) pretzel you use. When dipping the bite size Bavarian pretzels, it is easier and less time consuming to drop them in your melted coating by the hand full. I usually melt two pounds of coating and have my pretzels piled in front of me (all whole ones, reserve the broken ones for pretzel clusters).

Put a hand full into the melted coating and gently stir the coating so every pretzel is coated. Using your dipping fork (I prefer to use the handle of a paintbrush and insert it into one of the pretzel loops), lift each pretzel from the coating and drag it over the rim of your bowl to remove excess coating. Place it on a waxed paper-covered tray.

Large Bavarian pretzels can be dipped individually either by hand or by using a dipping utensil. Stick pretzels should be held by hand and dipped ¾ the way, or, using a shallow pan, rolled into the coating to cover the entire piece. Use a regular table fork to scoop the pretzel up and place on waxed paper.

Pretzels can be decorated with nuts, non-pareils, sprinkles, jimmies, colored sugar, or candy confetti for extra fun. You must sprinkle these things on before the coating sets. After you have a couple of rows of pretzels, stop, decorate, and then continue. Work in a nice organized rhythm at a steady pace or you will end up like "Lucy."

If you can dip a pretzel, why not a potato chip? You can, and they are great! Just like putting ketchup on anything so your kids will eat it at the dinner table, you can put coating on just about everything. Other things you might try are: popcorn, marshmallows, cookies, peppermint sticks, graham crackers, and ice cream cones. Be adventurous, dare to dip!

Working With Candy Centers

When you dip candy centers (caramel, truffles, mint, etc.), let them set at room temperature for a half an hour. This will make the outside of the center slightly crusty and will help to keep its shape when dipped into the melted coating. After you have dipped your candy and placed it on the tray to set, make a swirl on top of it with your dipping fork.

Tips...Tricks... and Interesting Stuff

The design or type of swirl that many manufacturers put on the top of a dipped candy is indicative of what type of center it has; to give a professional air to your candies, be imaginative and consistent.

Tips...Tricks... and Interesting Stuff

Dipped Truffles

The most basic truffle is a rich ganache (a stiffened cream made by the combination of heavy cream and chocolate) that is shaped into irregular small balls and then rolled in cocoa powder (a chocolate replica of the endeared and expensive black fungus truffle it was named after). Enriched with liquors, butter, and spices or enrobed in coating, the variations are infinite. If you love truffles, a great book to get is *Oh Truffles by au Chocolat,* written by Pam Williams and Rita Morin, it has page after page of wonderful recipes.

Bittersweet Ganache
16 ounces bittersweet chocolate/compound coating
1 cup heavy cream

Note: You do not have to temper your chocolate or white confectioner's coating to use in the ganache, but you do have to temper the chocolate or white confectioner's coating the truffle will be dipped in.

Pour heavy cream in a small saucepan and place on stove over a low flame. Keep a close watch on the cream because it comes to a boil rapidly. When you see small bubbles starting to form around the sides, remove the pan from the stove. Place your coating into the cream and stir while the coating melts. When all the coating is melted and blended in with the cream, pour the hot ganache into a bowl and place in the refrigerator for approximately one hour to cool. When the ganache is cool and stiff, either by hand or using a tablespoon, spoon out a small amount of ganache and roll it between your hands to form balls. Place the balls on a tray lined with waxed paper and return to the fridge until ready to dip. Dip your truffles one at a time in your 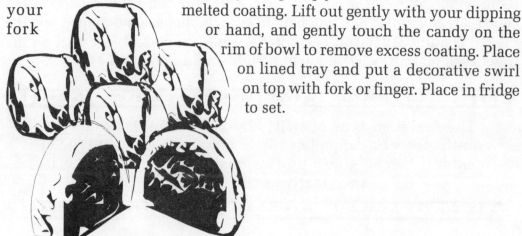 melted coating. Lift out gently with your dipping fork or hand, and gently touch the candy on the rim of bowl to remove excess coating. Place on lined tray and put a decorative swirl on top with fork or finger. Place in fridge to set.

Chapter

7

Incredible
Edible
Containers

Eating Your Plate

Putting a dessert into a container that you can eat instead of throwing away gives new meaning to the saying "having your cake and eating it too;" now you can "have your plate and eat it too!" Paper or foil cupcake liners, aluminum foil, jars, cups, bowls, balloons, and even cabbage leaves, can be used to make a mouth watering array of candy containers. These containers can be filled with fruit, mousse, or any other favorite dessert; they will certainly be devoured before you can take your place at the table.

Manufactured Molds

There are many types of molds designed to be used as receptacles; pour boxes are one of my favorite types. These molds can be either open (just a bottom) or covered (a top and bottom). They are available in different sizes and shapes to fit every occasion. There are of course, squares, circles and hearts; but there are also Christmas trees, Thanksgiving turkeys, and American flags. I even have one that is in the shape of the front of a house (I use this one as a "welcome to your new home" gift). No matter which one you use, each can be filled with an assortment of delicious goodies.

Seven years after our son Dominick, was born, we were blessed with Stephanie and Samantha, our twin girls. Well, all sense of control in our home was lost. You would have thought a child had never been born in our home (or the universe for that matter). Jessica, who was fourteen at the time, was ecstatic to finally have not one, but two sisters. Twelve year old Eddie consoled Dominick, who could not comprehend the injustice of having two babies, and not one of them being a little brother. Our new additions were not just babies, but dolls to dress up and fuss over; everything was lace, ribbons, ruffles, and bows. The balance had shifted from blue to pink in the Haufsk household!

It was no surprise, then, that the reception for the twins' Christening would rival any wedding. We had one hundred-twenty-five guests at the party; an occasion such as this definitely required chocolate. There were twelve tables that needed centerpieces, not to mention favors for the guests, and of course, the dessert table...Weeks before the big day I started molding. I would prepare chocolate in between feedings and emerge from my candy room hours later only wanting to sleep...oh gentle sleep...

The party was a huge success. Towards the party's end, the guests lingered. At first I did not give this much thought, after all it was a good party, but there were people sitting at the tables as if waiting for the others to leave. It was when Brenda, a close friend, approached me and asked, "who gets the carousel?" that I realized everyone was waiting to be the last person at the table to be able to take the centerpiece home.

The centerpieces were chocolate carousels made from *Life of the Party's #M-72 ABC Carousel*. The five ponies were poured in white coating and embellished in our color theme of deep lavender, teal and magenta. The top was decorated with tiny purple chocolate bows, and the carousel sat on top of a container filled with candy hearts. They were individually wrapped in clear cellophane and tied with curled ribbons and balloons to match the painted ponies. The favors that the guests received were tiny pour boxes in the shape of a baby carriage, *Life of the Party's* #B-40 Carriage Pour Box. The top was decorated with details of the carousel, with tiny hearts and the word "baby." These were also poured in white coating with the hearts and "baby" painted to match our theme colors.

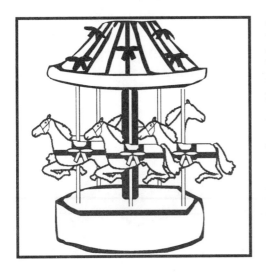

As impressive as all this may sound, I was not "Super Mom." (Pooped-out Mom was more like it!) These show-stopping centerpieces and favors were remarkably easy to make. Since I was making pieces in quantity, I used the assembly-line method and it proved to be my salvation. Note: You will need to have more than one mold, or you will go mad!! I had seven pony molds, and each mold had four ponies on it, so I could paint 28 ponies and pour them all at the once. While the ponies were being painted, the top and bottom pieces of the carousel were being poured and then refrigerated (these took longer to set because they were six inches in diameter and rather deep). After all the pieces were painted, poured, and set, the carousels were then assembled. Since the pour boxes required very little painting (the bottoms required none) I did them in between the stages of assembling the carousels. Each carousel weighed 1½ pounds; the container it sat on weighed one pound; the favors, three ounces.

Candy Cups

Not all molded pieces need to be as elaborate as these. A scoop of ice cream nestled in a bittersweet candy cup will have even the adults singing…"Ice cream, you scream, we all scream for ice cream." The amount of detail on your candy cup depends on the receptacle you use to mold it.

Cupcake Liners

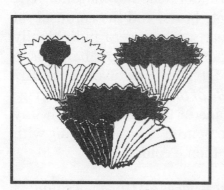

Cupcake liners are great to use because they are easy, economical and fun. You can use either the foil or paper type. The foil type can be squished and dented to add more character to your cups. First, line up your cups. Spoon your melted coating into the liner and spread the coating up the liner on all sides, making sure not to go over the rim or it will be hard to peel from the coating. Refrigerate to set. These cups will be thin and fragile; to make them more sturdy, you may want to give them a second coat after they have set. Do not let them get over-chilled or they will crack. After they have set, gently peel the liner from the coating. These cups can be made ahead of time, properly stored, and they will keep indefinitely.

Balloon Cups

The only problem you may encounter with this technique is keeping the kids from taking off with your balloon supply. I make it a point to have extras on hand so the kids will be occupied. Blow up your balloon, securing the opening with a clip, string or rubber band to prevent the air from escaping; this will allow you to untie it when you need to remove the balloon from your coating. Take your secured balloon and submerge the rounded end about three inches into your melted coating. Place the balloon in an upright position on a piece of waxed paper. To prevent it from falling over you will have to hold onto it for a minute until it starts to set. The alternative is to place a dollop of coating on the waxed paper before dipping your balloon (this will give it time to set a bit) and then place the balloon on it to keep it erect. Either way, after the coating has set, repeat the

procedure again to make a sturdier cup. When the coating has completely set, gently release the air and peel the balloon away from your cup. The excess coating that settled at the bottom will have formed a base to keep the cup standing. If you angle the balloon and coat each side one at a time, you can make cups in a variety of shapes. Experiment, try different angles; even funny-looking ones taste great! You can tell everyone that you were "exercising your artistic expression in a free-form style."

Nests

A nest is a fun project to do with the kids. There is a lot of freedom in making this type of container, and almost anything goes. Just like the bird who flits around and gathers twigs, grass and string to form its nest, the kids love to dribble the coating to make the necessary "twigs" incorporated in this project. There are two ways to make a nest—simple and simpler.

The simple way is to start with a round cup made from coating. Any of the techniques we have discussed is fine. Next, take a large piece of waxed paper (kids get a little excited at this part) and, using a spoon, paintbrush or any small utensil, dribble the coating on the paper, making thick and thin lines. You do not have to be neat, after all, twigs come in all shapes and sizes and are rarely straight. After the coating sets, peel the twigs from the paper (yes, many of them will crack and break; this is fine). Attach the twigs onto the inside of the nest; you do this by applying drops of melted coating on the cup, placing the twigs in any and every direction. When you are done with the inside, turn the cup upside down and do the same to the outside.

A simpler way to create a nest is to make your twigs as described above, but rather than using a pre-made cup, use the inside of a cereal bowl as a form, and then attach the twigs to each other. Start by laying some twigs in the bottom of the bowl. Dribble some melted coating on the twigs and add more twigs. Continue dribbling coating and adding more twigs working your way up the sides of the bowl. You will need more twigs for this version. After you have formed a nice nest, let the coating completely set. Gently nudge the nest from the bowl. Now you can fill it.

Woven Baskets

A tisket, a tasket, I love my chocolate basket. One of the most spectacular desserts on a warm summer night is a chocolate basket overflowing with fresh fruit dipped in chocolate.

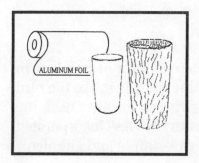

Making a basket is not difficult, but takes a little time; the basket has to be chilled in-between stages. The time can be reduced if you make several small baskets simultaneously. You can use any jar, cup, custard dish or bowl as the form for the basket, so long as the top or mouth of the container is wider than its bottom (this enables you to slip the basket off the form without breaking it). I prefer to use disposable drinking cups for my baskets, they work great. Lay the container on a piece of aluminum foil cut large enough to cover the sides and be tucked over the rim. Smooth the surface of the foil from the bottom and up the sides of the container.

Fill a piping bag with melted coating and hold the container upside down (put your hand inside it). Start to pipe coating onto the bottom of the container in circles, working your way from the outside toward the center. Pipe vertical lines from the edge of the bottom rim down the sides towards the top rim. Place in the refrigerator to set. If you are making more than one basket, start the next one now and alternate taking them in and out of the refrigerator as they set. Go over the lines you made on the basket to reinforce them and give them more definition. Do not worry about the lines all being the same width or perfectly straight, remember, baskets, like twigs, have character. Return the basket to the fridge. After the coating has set, start piping horizontal lines around the sides of the basket. You

will notice how the vertical lines give the illusion that the basket has been woven. Chill, and then go over the horizontal lines again. Chill again to set. After the basket is completely set, gently unfold the foil from around the rim. Ease the foil and basket off the glass in one piece. Gently peel the foil away from the basket. Now all you have to do is fill it and enjoy!

Journey to the Cabbage Patch

The molded cabbage leaf is so versatile, it was hard for me to decide in which chapter it should be included; you can use the leaves as bowls or garnishes. As a dessert, you can use some of the smaller leaves and fill them with mousse to create a dessert to die for. As a garnish, the leaves can be arranged and then connected with a dab of melted coating (like you did for brussels sprout roses) and placed right on top of a cake. You can then place a scoop of strawberries or raspberries in the center; either way they are incredibly easy to make. Take note, though, because of the moisture in the leaf, the finished piece will not have a glossy finish, but rather a matt finish.

Remove a few unblemished, firm, cabbage leaves from the head; wash and thoroughly dry them. You will be coating the **inside** of the leaf. Pour about a half cup of melted coating directly into the leaf and spread it to cover the entire surface, being careful not to overlap the coating on the edges or it will be difficult to peel. After the coating has completely set, gently peel the leaf away from the coating.

Boxes

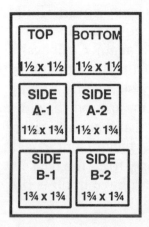

TOP 1½ x 1½	BOTTOM 1½ x 1½
SIDE A-1 1½ x 1¾	SIDE A-2 1½ x 1¾
SIDE B-1 1¾ x 1¾	SIDE B-2 1¾ x 1¾

The pieces of a box can be made using the technique used for silhouettes, or by using cookie cutters. You can also cut very straight lines by hand. It is important to cut your pieces to the specific size, they will not fit together correctly if the are not proportional to each other. To form a square box, you need to have six squares of candy (top, bottom, the same size; two facing sides the same size; the two other facing sides the same size). You will secure the sides together with melted coating.

First place the bottom piece on the counter. Take one side piece, apply a thin line of coating with a paintbrush (or pipe a line of coating) on the inside bottom edge of the side piece and secure it to the bottom piece. Continue this procedure for all sides.

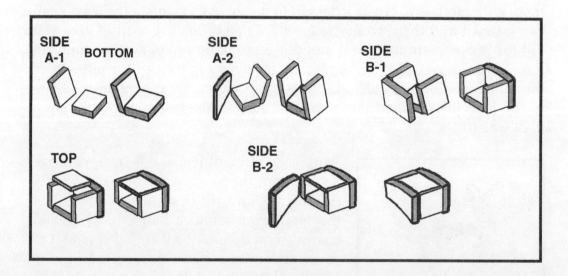

Chapter

8

Chocolate
Play Dough

Playing With Dough

Every mother knows (or woes) the creative achievements brought forth by our loving children and their play dough. My son Dominick loves the stuff so much that we had to start producing our own (refer to *"For Kids Only!!"* chapter 10, for the recipe). When I first heard about a "chocolate play dough" I knew it was something that would be welcome in my home.

Chocolate Play Dough is referred to by various names. Modeling chocolate, plastic chocolate, candy clay, modeling paste and flexible chocolate. They are all basically the same, the differences being the type of liquid mixed with the coating, either light corn syrup or glucose, and the amount of liquid added in relation to the amount of coating. My personal preference is to use 1½ teaspoons of syrup to every ounce of coating. You can also purchase ready-made chocolate play dough: *Albert Uster Imports Inc.* offers both dark and white *Modeling Paste from Carma* available in 13.2 pound plastic buckets.

Recipe for One Pound of Chocolate Play Dough
16 ounces coating
8 tablespoons of light corn syrup

Melt your coating either in a double boiler or in the microwave (you do not have to temper chocolate or white confectioner's coating). Heat the corn syrup but do not let it come to a boil. If you are using a white coating and want to add color to it, put your coloring into the corn syrup and mix thoroughly. You can also flavor your corn syrup with raspberry, coffee or any other flavor you desire simply by putting a couple of drops of an essential oil into the syrup. Slowly start mixing the warm corn syrup into the coating; it will start to stiffen and may look a little bit oily. After the coating is completely mixed, transfer the dough into a bowl and put into the fridge to cool. Chocolate Play Dough can be used as soon as it is cool enough to manage or it can be stored in the refrigerator in an air tight container for several weeks. If you store your dough, make sure you bring it to room temperature before use.

The dough will be quite stiff; if it is too hard you may have to warm it just a tad in either the microwave or warm oven. Knead the dough on the counter to make it more manageable, break off enough to work with, and cover the rest with a plastic wrap or aluminum foil (to prevent it from drying out). Now the fun can begin.

To get acquainted with your play dough, pretend you are one of your kids. Roll it, cut it, form it into balls, and make a play dough rope. Practice breading it, twisting it and bending it until you feel comfortable with it. If you have any molds, lightly dust the inside with some cornstarch and press the dough inside them. Turn the mold upside down and give it a little twist and your molded dough pieces should pop right out. Put them in the fridge to set and give them to the kids for a treat.

Tips...Tricks... and Interesting Stuff

The pieces you make will only be pliable for a short time. Chocolate Play Dough will completely harden like regular molded coating within a day or two.

Tips...Tricks... and Interesting Stuff

Ribbons and Bows

Finding the perfect gift for someone, often takes less time and thought than wrapping it does. We search for the perfect paper, ribbons and bows, and little decorations to put on the bows to thrill and excite the senses, even before the present is opened. Imagine the excitement you can arouse by gift wrapping your dessert...in chocolate!

When you hand your hostess a cake that is gift wrapped with chocolate ribbons and bows, the initial reaction is that it is not real. Then she smells that sweet chocolate aroma, touches and then tastes the decoration, and the rest is music to your ears...applause, applause, applause!

A single color ribbon or bow will make an attractive addition to your cake, but you will probably want to make multi-colored ones for a drop-dead gorgeous display. I will demonstrate making a two colored ribbon and bow using dark and white coating. After you have mastered this technique, you can make your ribbons and bows as wide or as narrow as you like, varying the colors by tinting white coating, and making multi-colored ribbons and bows by adding extra strands.

1. Make a batch of white chocolate play dough and a batch of dark chocolate play dough.
2. Make a rope about 12 inches long with the dark dough.

3.   Place the rope in between two pieces of waxed paper approximately 24-inches long.

4.   Using a rolling pin, roll the rope out flat into a long rectangular shape. It should be about ⅛ of an inch thick.

5.   Gently lift the top piece of paper off the dough and place it back on again (we just wanted to unstick it) and gently flip the papers and dough over. Gently remove the top paper (which formerly was the bottom), and set a side.

6.   Take a sharp knife and cut the long edges of the ribbon making sure they are straight lines. Cut the ribbon lengthwise into long thin strips (about ¼ to ½ inch wide). NOTE: Using a clear plastic ruler as a guide makes this part much easier.

7.   Cover the ribbon (to prevent drying) and set aside.

8.   Using the dough made from the white coating, follow directions 1-7.

9.   Gently take one of the white ribbons and lay it lengthwise very snug against one of the dark ribbons.

10.   Cover with waxed paper. Using your rolling pin, roll out the ribbon again until the dough is half its original thickness.

11.   Gently lift the top piece of paper off the dough and place it back on again (again, just to unstick it) and gently flip the papers and dough over. Gently remove the top paper (which was the bottom) and set aside.

12.   Trim the lengthwise edges in straight lines. You should have a thin, two colored ribbon approximately 18-inches long.

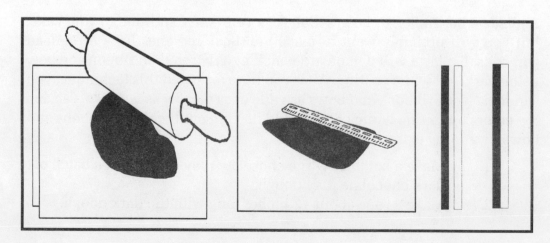

Assembling a Ribbon and Bow

Before you make your bow, place any ribbons you want on your cake. Gently pickup a ribbon, and starting at the bottom of the cake, go up one side, drape over the top and ease on down the other side. To make a bow, cut ribbons into the following pieces: two 6-inch strips; two 5-inch strips; and one 3-inch strip. Fold each of the 6 and 5-inch strips in half and pinch the ends together to form a loop. Take the 3-inch piece and form it into a circle. Set them aside to harden. Take the 6-inch loops and place them on your cake with the pinched ends facing each other. Place the 5-inch loops on top of the 6-inch loops, securing them in place with a dab of melted coating. Secure the 3-inch circle with melted coating directly in the center of the other loops with the pinched end facing down. You now have a beautiful bow. You can arrange your loops in any fashion you like, experimenting with different length loops and positioning them in a circular fashion and adding layers.

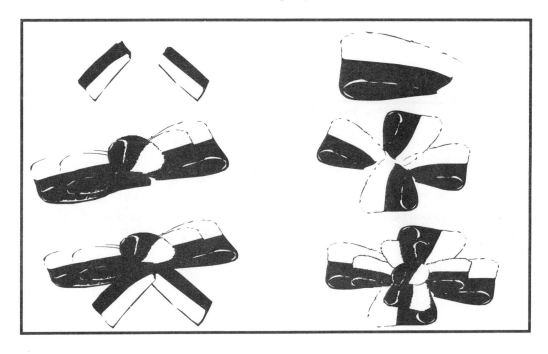

Fortune Cookies

I think the main reason my kids like to order Chinese food is so they can get fortune cookies. Now you can make your own and put your own little words of wisdom inside. I wonder if my daughter Jessica got one that said " you will have luck if your room is cleaned," it would have an impact on her...not! They make wonderful gag gifts with funny sayings or great pick me ups with words of encouragement inside. You can make a batch in several different colors and flavors; the possibilities are endless.

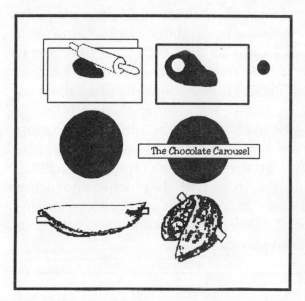

The Chocolate Carousel

Make your dough in the desired color and/or flavor. Using a rolling pin, roll out your dough to about ¼-inch thick. Using a round cookie cutter or narrow glass (about 2½ to 3-inches in diameter), press circles into your dough. Place one of your personal fortunes (paper should be approximately ½-inch wide by 3-inches long) in the center of each circle and fold circle in half. Press the edges together to seal them. Gently crease the cookie by bringing both ends together. Let set.

Flowers

Without a doubt, one of the most beautiful decorations is gum paste or sugar flowers. My hat goes off to all those talented people who recreate exquisite flowers so true to life that it is hard to imagine they are not real. Utilizing some of the techniques and supples that are used in sugar art, and with practice, you can make beautiful flower decorations with chocolate play dough.

You will need the following supplies: a template (refer to template section) or a flower cutter (these are similar to cookie cutters but much smaller and come in different petal shapes and sizes); a ball tool (a small stick with a rounded or pointed end used to help flatten and curl petal edges); a rolling pin and petal dust. Petal dust is a very fine colored powder which is applied with a small paintbrush.

The Rose

You should look at a picture of a rose before you start. Notice how it is formed in different layers and how the center of the rose is usually darker in color than the petals which surround it. The petals become much lighter with each layer. You can achieve this effect with coating two ways. You can make the rose one color of coating and then add color to it by brushing the petals with petal dust, or you can assemble the rose using different shades of dough. We will use both methods to create our rose.

Make three half pounds of dough using white coating. Tint each with a candy color making each a shade darker than the next. You now have three balls of dough in three different shades. You will be making a center piece and seven small petals from the darkest dough, three medium petals from the medium shade dough and five large petals from the lightest shade of dough. Keep all the dough covered in plastic wrap or aluminum foil when not in use.

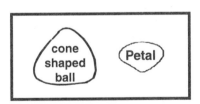

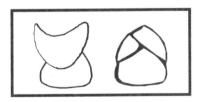

Pinch off a small piece of the darkest dough (about a ½-teaspoon full) and roll it into a cone shaped ball (like a candy kiss). Using the smallest rose petal cutter or template, make seven petals out of the darkest dough. Take one petal and, starting a little bit up from the bottom of the cone, wrap it around the cone overlapping the edges. Starting at the base of the cone, take another petal, wrap it half the way around the cone. Place another petal on the opposite side of the cone and wrap it in the other direction. Take the next four petals and wrap them around the cone individually, overlapping each other. Next take the three medium sized petals and flatten the edges and bend the edges outward with the ball tool. Place these petals gently around the cone, securing them at the base but keeping the outer

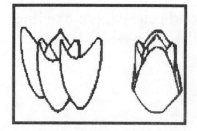

edges of the petals away from the cone. Do the same thing for the five large petals, bending the edges even farther away from the cone. You now have a beautiful rose; put it in the refrigerator to harden. Next, using a fine paintbrush, apply a small amount of petal dust to the edges of the petals which gives the rose a realistic effect.

Calla Lilies and Pine Cones

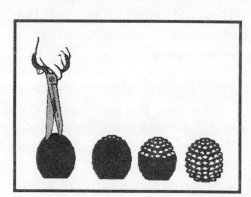

Two rather easy and attractive things to make are pine cones and calla lilies. To make a pine cone, form an oblong cone and place it on a lollipop stick or toothpick. Let it sit until firm but not completely hardened. Starting at the top, use the tips of small scissors to make a row of small cuts into the cone; push the cuts away from the cone. Continue making rows of cuts all the way down the cone in a shingle effect. Let the cones harden.

To create a calla lily, make three batches of dough, white, yellow, and green. Take a small amount of yellow dough and form it around a lollipop stick to form the stamen. Using the lily template or a lily petal cutter, make the petal and wrap it around the stamen as shown. Make leaves out of the green dough from a template or leaf cutter and wrap them around the base of the petal. Set to harden.

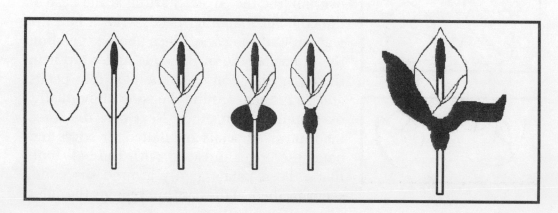

Fruits and Vegetables

Some of the easiest things to make with chocolate play dough are fruit and vegetables. You will have no trouble getting your kids to eat their veggies when they are made from chocolate. Imagine making a cornucoupia from chocolate and filling it with apples, grapes, lemons, limes, oranges and bananas all made from chocolate!

Oranges

Using orange colored dough, form into a ball. Make the skin true to life (dimpled) by gently rolling the "orange" on the fine side of a cheese grater. Insert a whole clove into one end to simulate the stem.

Bananas

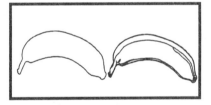

Using yellow dough, form a hotdog shape (slightly curved). Pinch each end to square them and insert a clove star into each end. Using petal dust paint brown lines down the banana lengthwise.

Berries and Grapes

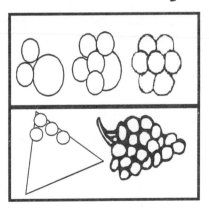

Color dough red, purple or green. You will need to make a small ball and many tiny balls in order to make a berry cluster. Secure the tiny balls onto the small ball with a dot of melted coating. For grapes, you will only need to make many tiny balls. You will have to form a triangular bottom layer and stack the "grapes" on top of each other, securing with a dab of melted coating to form a bunch.

Peaches

Use a light peach color dough. Form into a ball. Using the blunt edge of a knife, gently indent a line down one side of the "peach" and indent the top. The bottom should be slightly pointed. Use pink petal dust to "blush" the peach

Apples

Make red, green or yellow apples by tinting your dough that color. Shape your dough into a ball. Dent the top and bottom of the "apple." Place the stem of a whole clove in the top to form the stem and the clove star in the bottom to form the calyxes. Use petal dust to add spots or extra color.

Lemons and Limes

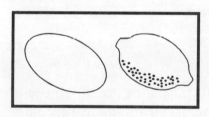

Make yellow dough for lemons and green for limes. Form into an elongated ball. Pinch each end with your fingers to form squared tapered ends. Gently roll your "lemon" or "lime" over a fine grater to dimple skin. Place a clove star into each end.

Carrots

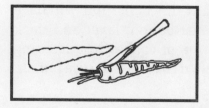

Using orange dough make a rope. Roll one end of rope into a point. Make some leaves out of green dough or use pieces of green licorice laces and place at the top of the "carrot." Use a butter knife to make indentations around the "carrot."

Chapter

9

The
Finishing
Touches

Special F-X

I use the mold, *Life of the Party #C-74 Large Santa Pop, to* make an old fashioned Santa face lollipop. I do not paint anything on the pop except for the small holly and berry design that is on his hat, and then pour him in milk or dark coating. Although he makes a simple but elegant addition atop a Christmas gift (which is the reason many of my friends ask me to make him), I always felt he was missing something…that twinkle in his eyes…so I put it there. I purchased non-toxic, metallic petal dust in gold and bronze, and then lightly brushed the surface of the pop with a paintbrush dipped into a mixture of the two. The result was awesome! His face seemed to come alive, and I have been making him that way ever since. People are amazed by this special effect.

All That Glitters and Even Gold

Petal dust comes in many colors and is easily applied to molded candies using a fine, soft bristled paintbrush. A little goes a very long way, so it must be used sparingly and with caution. The dust is so fine that it will fly in the air and land on anything close by; move to an area away from anything else you don't intend to dust.

When I make Christmas sleds, I brush the rails with bronze petal dust to give them an authentic appearance. If you are making a house and brush the windows with an opalescent dust, it gives the illusion of the reflection of real glass.

Edible glitter is available in clear or color. It can be sprinkled on your molded pieces to give the illusion of snow, ice and sequins. I have a lollipop mold of a snowflake on which I use this. I make all my pops and then quickly run a blow dryer over the surface to melt the coating just enough to enable the glitter to adhere to the pop. You can sprinkle glitter on roof tops, window sills and to accent a detail on any molded piece.

One of the neatest things I discovered was *Bombasei printed transfer sheets* available through *Albert Uster Imports, Inc.* They come in strips or sheets of plastic with gold colored stars or flecks (made from cocoa butter) printed on them. To use, spread your melted coating on the transfer sheet and let set. Cut into desired shapes and sizes; when the coating has completely set, peel off the plastic. The stars or flecks are transferred to the coating, leaving a most unusual and attractive creation.

 Gold leaf makes quite a statement when added to coating. When you purchase edible gold leaf, make sure it is between 22 and 24 karat. It is available in most art supply stores, and comes either patent, which needs to be cut with scissors, or loose, like petal dust.

Candy Canes and Peppermint Sticks

When I practiced hairdressing and theatrical make-up, I kept a "morgue." A morgue is a term which refers to files of pictures of different anatomical features. For example, I had a file of noses in all different shapes, sizes, ages and nationalities. I could refer to these pictures when I had to recreate someone's face to fit a particular character they were going to portray. I have carried this idea over to my candy room. I keep a "morgue" of carousels, Fabergé eggs, storybook characters, collectibles and other pictures I think I may be recreating in coating. I have a binder in which I keep many pictures, and have wallpapered my cabinets and refrigerator with others.

Through the use of my "morgue," I stumbled upon the use of candy canes. One day I saw a picture of a carousel made from gingerbread in which candy canes were decoratively placed on its top. I decide to make a similar carousel of chocolate with candy canes on top. It came out great. Candy canes come in many sizes, widths, colors, and even flavors. I've used the large thick ones to support the top in the center of a carousel, and the peppermint stick type (instead of lollipop sticks) to attach the ponies to the carousel.

It's a Wrap!

Your psyched! You've just finished making the most outrageous chocolate candy...now what? You can't just bring it to someone's house like it is...it must be wrapped or something...The way you wrap, package, or present your chocolate can make or break your chocolate, literally and figuratively.

There are many materials available to "package" your candies: cellophane bags, polypropylene bags, cardboard boxes, cellophane wrap, foils, plastic containers, baskets and tins. There are also several factors to consider in determining which material you will use to package your candies: health laws and state regulations, the size of the candy, how and where it is going, availability, cost, and presentation.

All Tied Up

As you know, my first experience with molding candy was making lollipops. I molded them and put them in poly bags sealed with transparent tape. Not too pretty, but it did keep them closed. When my girlfriend Fran saw them, she burst out laughing and suggested I use curling ribbon instead. This simple suggestion did the trick; the curling ribbon dressed up the pop, was easier than the tape, and could be color coordinated to fit any occasion. I have a peg board in my candy room with spools of every color ribbon imaginable. There is a store on Long Island called *Patchogue Floral;* which carries a large assortment of ribbons, many imprinted with different sayings, i.e., Merry Christmas, Get well soon, It's a Boy/Girl, Happy Birthday. There is probably a similar type store near you, if not, the address for Patchogue Floral is in the reference section of this book.

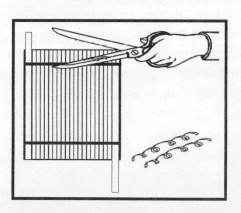

Using curling ribbon to tie your lollipops is decorative and easy, but it can be time consuming if you are making large quantities and have to cut and tie each of them individually. To save time, I curl ribbons while watching TV or talking on the phone using this method: Take a flat board (heavy cardboard is fine) eight inches long, wrap the ribbon around about fifty times, secure with a rubber band. Cutting straight across at both the top and bottom, you have just cut one hundred, eight-inch ribbons. What a time-saver! Curl each ribbon by scraping the sharp edge of a knife or scissor across its surface. If you are using printed ribbon, make sure you scrape the side that is not printed. Store excess in a plastic bag for future use.

When I make large molded pieces, I use longer pieces of several colors of ribbons, tied around the top with the strands cascading over the piece like ringlets. For party and wedding favors, I have ribbons specially made with the name, date, and occasion printed on them. I've had orange ribbons saying Happy Halloween printed in black, and pastel ribbons saying Happy Easter. They really dress up treats for special friends; although they cost about twenty-five cents a piece, they definitely make a statement!

Small, Medium and Xtra-Large

Finding bags and boxes to fit all your candies is sometimes like trying to fit a round peg in a square hole. Most candy suppliers carry a variety of bags and boxes made specifically for homemade candies. The most widely accepted item used to wrap lollipops are poly bags, which most suppliers stock in three popular sizes; 3x6, 3½x6 and 4x8; other sizes will usually have to be special ordered. I have found great success with these bags, the 3½x6 being the one that fits the majority of my lollipop molds. Do not try to squeeze a pop into a smaller bag; shards of coating will come off the sides of the pop and float around the bag, giving it an awful appearance. The length can always be trimmed to accommodate a wide but short piece of candy.

For large lollipops or small 3-dimensional molded candies, gusseted cellophane bags make wrapping a snap. These bags are crystal clear with a high shine and, because of the gusset, can accommodate an infinite range of candy sizes. The bags I use are the following sizes: 3½x2¼x7¾; 4x2¾x9; 5½x3¼x12; 6x3¾x14¾. Most of my molded candies can fit in one of these four sizes. I would love to find a larger cellophane bag to accommodate my carousel mold, if any of my readers have an idea as to where I might purchase them, definitely drop me a line—I'll personally thank you in my next book. My extra-large pieces, such as carousels, have to be wrapped. I accomplish this by using cellophane wrap that comes in rolls (like waxed paper does). I cut a piece that is large enough to cover the entire candy and be gathered at the top; I secure the top with ringlets of curling ribbon and then seal the sides with transparent tape.

Boxes come in a variety of shapes and sizes. There are clear acetate boxes; boxes with cardboard bottoms and clear tops; boxes with windows; flat folding boxes; boxes that come in the shape of hearts and Christmas trees;

tuxedo shaped boxes; purse boxes and ones that have inserts designed specifically to house particular molds.

Even though boxes are more costly than bags, some fragile or awkwardly shaped molded candies are better suited for a box than a bag. There is a mold of a familiar carrot-eating rabbit—the molded piece is tall and slender and can easily be broken—thank goodness there is a box in the same shape in which to package him. Truffles, to me, are a more impressive gift when packaged in a box; they keep fresh longer, too.

Health Laws and State Regulations

When you make gifts for friends or relatives it isn't necessary to concern yourself with laws and regulations. When you make candies to sell, however, there are some questions that will need to be answered and things you'll have to do to satisfy the local regulatory agencies, whether it be at fairs or through retail outlets. Check with your city officials as to regulations; your local chamber of commerce can tell you whom to contact. Health codes in your area may dictate what type of material you can use for packaging and also what ingredient labels are needed, etc.

Candy On The Fly

I frequently send candy via next day air to my Mother down in Florida; she always receives it in the same condition as I sent it. When sending coatings through the mail, the quickest way is usually the safest. You do not want your candy to be sitting somewhere for a week and reach its destination melted and/or broken. Another trick I have learned is to put an ice pack in the container in which you are shipping your candy; it helps prevent your candy from melting.

Presentation

There are many fairs and craft shows on the Island where I live; I have participated in a few and attended many. I always stop at the booths of people who sell candy, not only to buy it, but to see how they have displayed their wares. It never ceases to amaze me how little effort some vendors put into displaying their candy: bag it, plop it on the table and sit there waiting, as if the candy was going to sell itself. If the candy is extraordinary or the vendor has no competition it might, but more often than not, it requires an attention getter. With imagination and a few props, your candy can be as artistically displayed as the candy itself.

I once inquired about renting a space in a fair held annually at a prestigious school on the south shore. I had to submit a registration form with a detailed description of how I planned to display my candy, accompanied by a photograph of my booth for review to see if I qualified for acceptance. My first thought was, how absurd! I wasn't going to waste my time, but the thought intrigued me; I started wondering...oh how I wondered. My imagination kicked in and I started thinking of all kinds of crazy things and ways to display my candy!

After Christmas (at a 75 percent discount!) I purchased an "illuminated dimensional display." Translated, it is large tri-folded piece of cardboard with a scene on the front with miniature lights attached to it. It is supposed to be used as a background for displaying animated dolls, but it makes a fantastic display for candy. I improvised by replacing the miniature lights with the battery-operated kind, this way, the display would now be portable as there was no need for electricity or a cord. It sat securely at one end of the table with room to place the candy in front of it. The picture on my display is the front view of a house decorated for Christmas. Arranged in front of the display were Christmas trees, sleds, snowmen, presents, Santa, and, of course, a carousel, all made from coating. This type of display is not expensive, can also be handmade, and makes one heck of a presentation. By the way, although it prompted some new ideas for displays, I never did submit my registration form to the fair.

A lollipop stand is essential if you are going to display them. You can use Styrofoam, but it's more fun to use building blocks. The old fashioned wooden blocks, and empty spools of thread make great lollipop holders (and you thought they were just for kids). Arrange the blocks so they spell out a word, CANDY, HAPPY HOLIDAYS, THANKSGIVING, etc. Drill holes in the top to hold a few pops, then you can place this in front of your Styrofoam. The spools already have holes in them and can be painted and then glued together to form a unique arrangement.

I had my husband help me make a half dozen pop holders out of 2x4's. He drilled several rows of holes on the four-inch side and then painted them. We glued flat wooden figurines on the two-inch front side to coordinate with special holidays. Each stand cost only a couple of dollars and a little bit of time.

Chapter

10

For
Kids
Only!!

I'm Bored...There's Nothing To Do

When I was young and complained how bored I was and that there was nothing to do, my Mother would explain how fortunate I was, and then tell me how little, in comparison, she had as a child...you know, how she walked five miles in knee-deep snow to get to school...etc., etc. My childish reply was always that I would be different, that is, if indeed, I should ever have children. After non-stop complaints from my own five children, of "I'm bored there's nothing to do..."I find that I have become my Mother! If I hear I'm bored one more time, I'll definitely be committed!

Dominick's Play Dough

My candy room, then, became the equivalent of going to a therapist (but much less expensive). I could go downstairs with a cup of hot delicious coffee, turn on one of my "return-to-the-seventies" CDs and relax, making something beautiful in coating. My kids know that when Mom is making candy, she is not to be bothered. Right! Keeping them occupied is actually pretty easy. The twins come to the gate, which separates me from the rest of the world, hands stretched out, asking "chocit milk" (their way of saying "give me a piece of chocolate"). I ration out four chocolate discs at a time, thrilling them to no end. Dominick, though, isn't so easily pacified; however, he loves to play with play dough, and luckily can be occupied for hours at a time. I learned to make homemade play dough when he was in pre-school. It is easy, non-toxic, economical, and, best of all, washes out of everything! I let him pick out several molds from my collection and he happily amuses himself, allowing me to make my candy.

Dominick's Play Dough

½ cup salt   2 tablespoons of oil
1 cup flour   1 cup (colored) water
2 teaspoons of creme of tartar

To make the dough, combine all the ingredients in a small pot and stir to mix. Over a low flame, stir until the dough starts to get thick; it happens rather quickly. At this point, remove the pot from the heat source and continue to stir. It will be very thick. Spoon the dough onto a piece of waxed paper to cool. When the dough is cool enough to handle by hand, knead it to make it uniform. It is now ready to be played with. The dough will stay good for several weeks in an air tight container.

If you want your dough to be all one color, mix a couple of drops of food coloring into your water before adding it to the dry ingredients. If, however, you prefer to have several colors, divide your dough in half, thirds, or quarters then knead the color into each pile.

Eddie's Party

My son Eddie's birthday falls during the winter break from school. I always had a hard time figuring out what to do for his party. Many of his friends would be away on vacation and the weather would often be unpredictable. Finding something to do with a room full of little boys was always a challenge, until I decided to have a "candy party." Each child could create his own candies and decorate them any way he wanted. The boys were occupied, had a lot of fun and got to bring home all the goodies they made.

Having a "candy party" is a wonderful idea for both girls and boys, from five years old to ten. Adult supervision is an absolute must, though, because you will have to melt and pour the coating. The children gather around the table and each one is given a mold and a paintbrush or lollipop stick. They dip their paintbrush into bowls of colored coating set on a warming tray positioned in the center of the table. After they have colored their molds, you pour the coating in and place the molds in the refrigerator to set; the children meanwhile can enjoy cake and ice-cream. When the candy is set the children can wrap their treats to take home. Place the candy in goodie bags and off they go!

You can also make Dominick's play dough as a party theme and let the children help make their own play dough to take home (making sure the parents don't mind first). Another variation of Dominick's play dough is the type that you let harden for making decorations or ornaments.

Dominick's Ornament Dough

½ cup salt   ⅔ cup water
2 cups flour

Mix all the ingredients in a bowl using a large spoon or your hands. When the ingredients are thoroughly combined, remove the dough from the bowl and knead on the counter to remove any remaining lumps.

The dough can either be pressed into a mold or rolled out with a rolling pin; shapes can then be pressed into it with cookie cutters. While the dough is soft, press a paper clip or ornament hook into the back of each piece making sure it extends above the top. Let the ornaments dry for a couple of days, then paint them with water colors and decorate with glitter, rhinestones or sequins. You can even give them a shiny coating using clear nail polish.

Any of your candy molds can be used for the above recipes. Imagine the delight your child will have from making wonderful ornaments for your Christmas tree, or presents that they can give to their friends (and you).

More Neat Stuff

There are many things that the children can participate in when it comes to the kitchen. One thing springs to mind that is fun and has the most intelligent adult thinking "how did they do that?" is chocolate eggs.

Chocolate Eggs

Chocolate eggs in a real shell, are so cool, but require some adult participation. The next time you want to prepare eggs for breakfast (or just plan on having a scrambled egg feast), do not break the eggs; instead make a small hole in the top and bottom of the egg with a toothpick or large hat pin. You guessed it, have the children blow the egg out of the hole keeping the shell in tact. After all the egg has been removed, carefully rinse the inside with water (a small stream from the faucet does the trick), then blow in the holes again to remove most of the water. Let the shells air dry too remove any trace of moisture. After you have several clean, dry empty egg shells, melt your coating and put it into

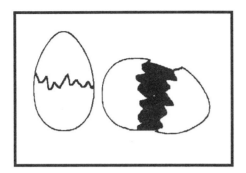

a decorating bag with a small holed tip. Pipe the coating into the empty egg shell till it is full. Refrigerate to set. If you used milk or dark coating, you can hide the holes by dabbing a dot of white coating over them. Now you have what appears to be an egg but is really chocolate!

Monkeying Around With Bananas

Each Fall, my husband makes several trips Upstate; he always stops at his friend's farm and brings home a large bag of apples (he loves apple pie). In between making apple pies, making caramel and candy apples has become a fall tradition. We do not make them at any other time of the year, instead, we make chocolate bananas.

Chocolate bananas are easy, fun and nutritious. Push a pop-sickle or lolli-pop stick into one end of the banana. If you peel down only part of the skin and hold on to the unpeeled part, this task is easier. Holding on to the stick, dip the banana into a bowl of melted coating. Before the coating sets, sprinkle the banana with chopped nuts, coconut flakes, crispy cereal or any other topping you have at hand. Chocolate bananas are like a banana sundae without the ice cream.

Chocolate Pizza

Having a pizza party is always fun but having a chocolate pizza party is fantastic. This is another great idea for a birthday party theme or works wonders for a pajama party. The trick hear is to cut the slices before the coating completely sets or place the finished "pie" in a warmed oven for a few seconds.

Pour melted milk chocolate coating into a pizza (or any other shallow) pan to about a 1/4 inch thick. Sprinkle anything and everything you want on top. Crispy ceareal, nuts, raisins, and small pieces of white coating are my favorites. Let set and watch those slices disapear!

Lending a Helping Hand

It has been my experience that children get great satisfaction from lending a helping hand; it has also been my experience that it is much easier and less traumatic (for them and for you) to find something with which they can help you, rather than to try and explain that their assistance is not needed.

During busy times, I delegate some of my responsibilities to my children. It is not difficult for the older children to bag candies or tie ribbons around them. I usually set a large tray in front of them and let them go to town. It makes them feel good that they have contributed to my effort and it saves me a lot of time. They also carry boxes of candy in and out of the candy room, transport them to the car, and help deliver them. My son Eddie is my biggest fan; he tells everyone that his Mom makes candy and always brings home a customer. My teenagers even make their own candy to give as small gifts to their friends at holiday time. My husband, Stephen, helps me when I get busy or when he gets lonely. He pays frequent visits to my candy room and has developed a flair for pouring coating. Making candy is a wonderful experience that can be shared with the entire family.

Chapter

11

Creating
Magical Gifts
from Chocolate

Magic

Mysteriously impressive; beautiful, is my favorite definition of magic. As you have learned in the previous ten chapters, anyone can be a magician and produce magical gifts from chocolate.

By now, you have tried all or most of the ideas in this book, but perhaps you are still struggling with unlocking your imagination. The following pages are filled with ideas and illustrations that will put your imagination in gear.

Christmas Magic

Christmas is probably my busiest time of year, I think I make more candy in December than I do for Valentine's Day and Easter combined. Many of my friends like to attach a small candy or lollipop to the ribbons on their gifts or use them as an extra stocking stuffer.

I have a friend whose father is in a nursing facility. She acknowledges every staff member who helps in the care of her father by giving them homemade candy for the holidays.

Christmas time and charities seem to go hand in hand, and it is often that I am called upon to make a special piece that can be used as a door prize or be included in a raffle.

From Our House to Yours

I love going into collectable shops, especially around the holidays. You can get so inspired by the way the shop owners display their collections. One of my favorites is the holiday villages; what could be more impressive than Dickens®, Christmas in the City®, or Sugar Town®? How about your very own village...in chocolate! A breathtaking presentation and gift all in one. Display your chocolate village on your table during your Christmas party and give each of your guests a piece to take home. You can construct a building utilizing the box technique in Chapter 7, *Incredible Edible Containers*, using a template from any gingerbread house pattern, the template in the reference section of this book, or by using a mold. You can make cobblestone streets using candy bars or a break a part mold (candy bar mold) and then line the streets with chocolate trees! A snowman or a sled filled with presents placed in front of a house, even a chocolate Santa can be sneaking down the lane, all made from your favorite coating. Following is a list of my favorites:

Tomric's Small Village Scene #756 through #766
Tomric's School House #767
Tomric's Village Store #768
Tomric's Town Hall #769
Tomric's Church #770
East Coast Molds Candy Store #AO-855, 1-3
Life of The Party's Accessories for Village #M-50
Life of The Party's Break-apart bar #AO-72
Tomric's Bar Mold #G-187
Tomric's Small Evergreen Tree #H-654
Tomric's Large Evergreen Tree #H-655

The Nutcracker Sweet

My daughter Jessica loves musicals and ballet. One of her favorites is *The Nutcracker Suite,* and she has seen several versions of this musical. If you have a Nutcracker Suite lover in your life, give them a chocolate version to see...and eat!

There are several ballerina, nutcracker soldiers and tree molds that you can choose from. I love *Tomric's Toy Soldier #H-653.* You can make a tree in white coating and decorate it with M&Ms or other small candy. If you want to get really elaborate, take green colored licorice laces and wrap it around the branches for lights and place dragees, M&Ms, or other small drop candy for light bulbs. Make presents and pile them around the base of the tree and place the nutcracker to one side and the ballerina on the other.

Sleigh Bells Ring

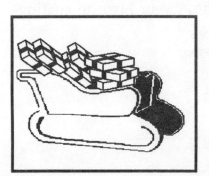

One of my new favorites (I have so many), is the large sleigh made by *Classic Design #C-73.* I love large molds and when they came out with this one, I just had to have it. It is large enough to put a dozen or two cookies piled high inside and is a spectacular gift to bring to a Christmas party. You can also place a chocolate Santa's bag filled with chocolate presents or Santa himself inside. This is one mold that definitely belongs in everyone's collection.

There are several different sleigh molds available in several sizes. You can also make one of your own using the techniques for silhouettes, cut outs and making a box. I make a small sled, approximately four inches long, that holds six chocolate presents inside. This piece is great for the numerous people you would like to give a little acknowledge gift to around the Christmas season. It is also a wonderful alternative to place cards used for seating arrangements.

Frosty

Another favorite mold is *Classic Design's #C-65 Snowman.* This mold was designed in such a way, that you can mold it as a semi-solid snowman or cut the hat portion of the mold off (in essence creating two separate molds) and make a chocolate cookie jar out of it. I make this piece as a cookie jar snowman. I pour the hat portion in dark or milk coating and the snowman's face in white coating. Fill it with a pound and a half of Christmas cookies or chocolate covered pretzels and this is one snowman everyone would like brought into their home.

Christmas Carousel

Every year requires an original idea for my Christmas carousel. My carousels have become a sort of moniker of my candy making. I use the *ABC carousel from Life of the Party #M-72,* more than any other mold in my collection. This carousel comes in three parts; a top with half a center pole, a bottom with half a center pole and a flat mold containing four ponies (however the completed carousel requires five). One Christmas, I poured the ponies in white coating, painted their saddles green and red, and placed a sugar wreath on each one. The center pole and bottom pieces were poured in milk coating and the top piece was poured in white. I placed ten small, red and white striped candy canes on the top and decorated the sides with small sugar decorations. The six inch diameter carousel fit perfectly on a clear plastic container that I use, that houses cookies, small candies, covered pretzels or a one pound bag of M&Ms quite nicely. Twenty-seven carousels wrapped in clear cellophane and tied with green, red, gold, and white ribbons, left my candy room that Christmas.

Tips...Tricks... and Interesting Stuff

If you have trouble keeping the ponies secured to the base, try securing a life saver type of candy on the bottom piece and putting the lollypop stick inside or pushing a gum drop type of candy onto the stick and securing it to the bottom.

Tips...Tricks... and Interesting Stuff

Thanksgiving Magic

It is funny what you choose to remember from your childhood; when I think of Thanksgiving, I think of nuts. My father loved all types of nuts, and after dinner and dessert was served, all the grown-ups sat at the table drinking their wine or sipping coffee, cracking nuts, while telling the greatest stories. Mom always had a huge bowl filled with every kind of nut imaginable and a half a dozen nut crackers placed in the center of the table; it was over cracked nuts, that I learned more about the history and escapades of my family. As an adult, I find it much easier to purchase the shelled variety and dip them in chocolate.

Most people associate Thanksgiving with turkey, stuffing and sweet potato pie, not chocolate. However, aside from chocolate covered nuts, there are many creative ways to incorporate chocolate into the Thanksgiving menu, below are a few of my favorite ways.

A Cornucopia of Thanks

Anytime I am in the Smithtown area, I stop at *Emily's Chocolate Shop*. I've known Emily for quite some time now and have acquired some unique molds from her to add to my collection. There was a mold company, that went out of business before I became involved with candy making, who made really outrageous molds; Emily happened to have several, and luckily, now, I do too!

One year, around Thanksgiving time, I stopped by her store to say hello. Emily had just finished filling the greatest chocolate cornucopia with cookies. I inquired about the mold that she had used to make it, hoping it was not one made by the company that went out of business and that I could get one. She told me it was *Tomric's #H-738* and ordered one for me. Unique in design, this mold makes a 2¾ pound cornucopia that can easily hold two pounds of gourmet cookies and makes the most spectacular centerpiece on anyone's Thanksgiving table.

Make a Wish

Breaking the wishbone, from the old belief that when pulled apart by two people, each making a wish, the one who gets the longer part will have his wish come true, has become more of a tug of war in our household. Having five children plus myself (Stephen, a nonbeliever) vying for the wishbone, left me wishing there was more than one. If your house is like my house, the dilemma of who gets the wishbone is easily rectified by everyone receiving one, you guessed it, in chocolate. *Life of the Party* makes a wishbone mold *#M-31*, that makes breaking the wishbone a snap! They also make a unique alternative to place cards. Make a wishbone for each guest tied with a ribbon and card with their name on it.

Turkey

There are dozens of turkey molds available and in just as many sizes. You can make a turkey centerpiece using one of the large molds, like Tomric's #H-827, a whopping twenty-five pounds of chocolate or use a one ounce turkey, Tomric's #H-688 and use them in place of seating cards at your dinner table.

Halloween Magic

It is a shame that this holiday has become one of the scariest, and not for the costumes, but for the safety of our children. I purchase closed bagged candy for my trick or treaters and reserve my homemade candy for my friend's children, otherwise it probably would get thrown away out of a parent's fear of not knowing where it came from or who made it.

As an alternative to door to door trick or treating, our community, like so many others, has organized trick or treating at the shopping mall and the elementary school. Another safe alternative is the old fashioned Halloween party at home. It is here that you can make the wonderful things from the past like, pop corn balls, Grandma's walnut fudge, homemade marshmallow crispy bars, s'mores, hot cocoa and hot apple cider. The following treats will definitely please any angel, monster, ghost or goblin that attends your Halloween party.

Bubble and Boil

There is a cauldron mold, *#H-40*, from *Life of The Party* which makes the best edible container for a Halloween bash. It is easy to make and can be filled with an assortment of treats. The best way to fill them is with the "witch's brew," a treat my boys think is wild. Make a cauldron for each guest and fill them with chocolate pudding. Sprinkle crumbled chocolate cookies on the top and place candy gummy worms and candy gummy frogs peaking out from the rim. They'll be a scream.

Come Into My Web

Using the technique for *piping coating* from *chapter 5, The Glory of Garnishing*, make spider webs using the template from the reference section of this book. Place one or two on individual cupcakes or arrange them on the top of a cake.

Halloween Carousel

Making a carousel with a Halloween theme was a fun project. I immediately thought of the story, *Ichabod Crane and the Headless Horseman*. All I could picture was that crazy man in a black cape riding that big black horse. I poured my carousel in milk chocolate. The ponies' saddles were painted in black and orange and they were poured in dark coating. I placed a small pumpkin on the back of each pony and secured candy corns to the base. I cut black licorice laces into eight pieces, long enough to cover the top of the carousel and hang over the sides about an inch. I then placed a half of a chocolate ball on top to make it look like the body of a spider. A couple of red dots for eyes and I had the perfect Halloween carousel.

Easter Magic

When my eldest children, Jessica and Eddie, were young, they're Easter baskets contained candy that they knew I did not make, like jelly beans, malted balls, and marshmallow chicks. It was frustrating to make all my beautiful candy for other people and not give it to my own children, for fear that they would question the identity of the Easter Bunny. However, the problem was solved by the time my third child, Dominick, started asking questions. Jessica and Eddie, by this time, were old enough to be my "holiday helpers" and told Dominick that Mom got a job helping the Easter Bunny fill his orders. Now all my children get Mom's special treats and long live the Easter Bunny!

There are so many wonderful molds available for Easter time. Chocolate baskets filled with an assortment of candies. Rabbits come in all shapes and sizes, my favorites are the *Pot Belly Rabbit , #H-743* and the *Mother*

Rabbit, #H-705, made by *Tomric.* The Pot Belly Rabbit is dressed in a top coat which I paint in a pastel color for Easter time and the Mother Rabbit has little bunnies clinging to her legs and in her arms. Both these molds can be colored to match other holidays like, Mother and Father's day, baby showers and retirement.

Although there are hundreds of molds available, and you know by now, I could go on and on about each one, I've limited myself to a few of my more imaginative ideas.

Panoramic Eggs

Almost every Sunday, our newspaper contains an advertisement from the *Franklin Mint or Bradford Exchange,* accompanied by a full page color picture. Whenever the offer is for a carousel, 3-dimensional plate, Fabregè Egg or panoramic egg, I cut it out and place it in my "morgue." These pictures are a great source of inspiration.

Life of The Party, makes an Easter egg mold *#E-202 Crystal Egg,* that I use to make a panoramic egg display. There are molds designed especially for panoramic designs, however, I like the crystal pattern on this particular mold. I cut out the center of the front piece of the mold, following the diamond shaped pattern. Instead of discarding the cut out piece, I fill it as I would a any flat mold and use it as a base for the egg to stand on. A pony from the *ABC Carousel* mold, fits inside the egg, as does an enormous amount of small 3-dimensional molded pieces. For Easter, I place a small 3-dimensional bunny inside, nestled on a bed of Easter grass and jelly beans.

Charitable Basket

One year, for a charity raffle, I made a 16-inch long chocolate Easter basket. Inside was *Tomric's #H-700, Large Duck,* weighing in at just over three pounds; surrounded by dozens of bite size candies. The elderly gentleman who was the proud recipient of this spectacular basket, remarked how his grandchildren were overjoyed with Grandpa's big treat.

Bunny Cookie Jar

Classic Design's #E175, Bunny Cookie Jar, is another mold that can be used for other occasions. It is designed the same way as their snowman cookie jar mold, which can be modified so it can be filled. Putting bows on the bunny's ears, it can be used for a little girls birthday and Mother's Day

or add a pair of spectacles and it is great for Grandparent's Day. *Tomric's #H-724, Pacifier* mold, placed on the face of the bunny, transforms it into a sweet centerpiece for a baby shower or welcome home treat for a new parent.

Easter Carousel

I like to use *Tomric's #G-493, Carousel,* for Easter time. The top, bottom, and three large ponies, have a lot of detail which can be painted. For Easter, I like to pour the carousel in white coating tinted a pastel color. The ponies manes and tails are painted in different pastel colors and then poured in white coating. Small candy flowers are scattered on the carousel base and top with a larger flower placed on each pony's saddle.

Valentine Magic

Valentine's Day will always have an extra special meaning for me because it was on that day, that Stephen asked me to marry him. A *Vermont Teddy Bear®* was delivered to my house, on one arm of the bear was a delicious box of truffles and the other arm supported a box containing an engagement ring. The card read "Will you marry me?" And of course I said yes, let him put the ring on my finger…then quickly ate the truffles!

Will you be my Valentine? These words are synonymous with chocolates or a bouquet of roses. You would think that Valentine's Day would be a very busy time for me and chocolate, but compared to the other big holidays, it is one of my slowest holidays. Because of this, I have limited my selection to a few special pieces.

Chocolate Roses

My most requested item for Valentine's Day is my boxed roses, using *Life of The Party's Long-Stemmed Rose #F-15.* There are three roses on this mold. I paint the flower a deep red, the leaves a dark green, and pour the rose in milk chocolate. I place six roses in a clear plastic long stem rose box and tie it all up with white ribbon imprinted with red hearts.

One year, at the dinner table, Stephen sensed that something was bothering me and asked if anything was wrong. I looked at him and said "I have to make 180 roses and I don't think I can get them all done tonight." It was the day before Valentine's Day and everyone I knew called my office asking if they could get a half dozen roses for the morning. I just kept saying yes and taking down names. By the end of the day, I had accumulated thirty orders. Needless to say, everyone in the family pitched in. I had ten molds, so I could paint thirty roses at a time. Stephen poured and the children wrapped. All the orders were filled, delivered, and everyone had a happy Valentine's Day.

Valentine Carousel

One day I received a call from a woman who wanted a carousel for Valentine's Day. She told me that a close friend of hers was feeling blue because it was the first holiday after her friend's divorce. Her friend loved carousels and thinking it might boost her spirits, the woman asked if I made a carousel for this holiday, I said "sure, why not." It was the first Valentine Carousel I made.

I poured the carousel in white coating and painted the details of the ponies in red and pink. I placed a large jelly heart on the saddle of each pony and smaller hearts all over the top of the carousel. Wrapped in clear cellophane and tied with ringlets of white, pink, red, and ribbon imprinted with the words "I love You" it was a delight to receive and eat!

And Baby Makes Three...

Well, in my case, seven! In the seventeen years that I have been a mother, I can honestly say that I have made more than my share of candy for showers, Christenings, and birthdays. My list doesn't stop with my children;

with children you get teachers, bus drivers and friends. Their friends have parents who have showers, Christenings and birthdays and the circle continues. There is always a child's occasion that can be made sweeter with homemade candy.

Building Blocks

I have never met a child, who at some point in their life, has not enjoyed playing with building blocks. You know, the kind made from left over pieces of two by fours from Dad's latest project, or bought at the neighborhood toy store with A B C printed on them, or the box filled with and played with at their first preschool, or the one you missed picking up and stepped on with your bare feet in the middle of the night...oh, those, now you remember! Those wonderful (hard on your feet) little blocks can be made in candy and used in an infinite variety of ways for a multitude of occasions.

There are several building block molds available, *Life of The Party* makes a three-inch block *#B-15, Baby Block and #B-17, Small Block.* You can also use the technique from *Chapter 7, Boxes*, to make any size block you need. Stack them on top of each other to spell "Baby" or "ABC" and use it as the center support for a carousel; or, make a few large blocks that spell out "Boy," "Girl," or even "Twins" and place small 3-dimensional pieces on top to make a one-of-a-kind centerpiece.

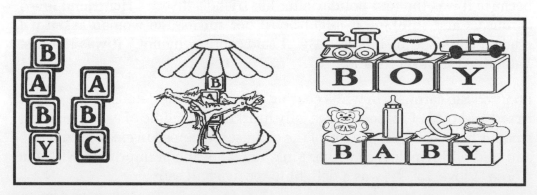

 I have a mold, which consists of several pieces that form a jack-in-the-box when it is assembled. Although this mold is no longer available, you can make something similar. Make a large block keeping the top opened, and then place a clown head, bear or any other 3-dimensional piece protruding from inside it.

Baby Bottles

Baby bottles come in all shapes and sizes now a days and many are incorporated in gift baskets filled with everything from jelly beans to wash clothes. For a unique shower favor or a delicious addition to a gift basket, make a 3-dimensional baby bottle out of chocolate from a mold like *Life of The Party's #B-37, 4 ounce Bottle; #B-38, eight ounce Bottle; or Tomric's #H-716, Baby Bottle.* Instead of making it solid, use *Method two* for *Semi-Solid or Hollow Candies, from Chapter 4, Making Molded Magic.* Place a few jelly beans inside the bottle before you combine the two halves together.

A Carousel for Every Occasion

The carousel featured on the front cover of this book and illustrated in detail in the following chapter was made freehand. Manufactured molds were incorporated, however, the main body of the carousel was made using the techniques from the previous chapters.

Utilizing your imagination, you can create a carousel, either by using manufactured molds or many other things in your home. By painting and adding accessories, you can make a carousel for any and all holidays or special events in your life.

Chanukah Carousel

My friend Marcie, is of the Jewish faith, and is married to a man who celebrates Christmas. During one holiday season, talking over raspberry truffle coffee and cookies (we both love flavored coffee), she remarked how she and her husband received many Christmas cards but rarely did she receive a seasons greeting card or Chanukah card from friends. Marcie always loved my candy, especially my carousels, and had planned on bringing one to her mother's home for their holiday dinner.

My first Chanukah carousel was made that year. Using the *ABC Carousel*, I poured the carousel and ponies in white coating. The details of the ponies were painted in blue and gold, the colors of Chanukah. Gourmet blueberry candy canes (they were blueberry flavored and blue in color) were arranged

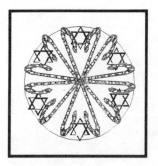

on the top of the carousel. Positioned the with the hook section facing up, just touching the outer rim of the top, and set on an angle so every two formed a "V." A chocolate Star of David (made from a bite-size mold) was placed in the center of each "V." The carousel was wrapped in clear cellophane and tied with white, blue, gold, and ribbons imprinted with Happy Chanukah on them. Needless to say, Marcie loved the carousel and greatly appreciated the thoughtfulness that went into such an original piece of candy.

Kwanzaa Carousel

Kwanzaa, occurring annually from December 26 to January 1, is a relatively new (established in 1966, by Maulana Karenga) but fast spreading celebration of fasting, feasting and self-examination. If you celebrate Kwanzaa or have a friend that does, making a carousel incorporating some or all of the symbols of Kwanzaa would be a welcome and delicious addition to the celebration.

The colors of Kwanzaa are black, red and green. You can use dark or milk coating and paint details in red and green. Thanksgiving molds, which have a variety of fruits and vegetables like pumpkins and corn, can be added to your carousel, keeping with the Kwanzaa traditions. You can also place bite-sized chocolate presents on the base of the carousel, poured in dark coating with the ribbons alternating (in representation of the kinara) red and green.

Carousel-Us-Rex

Although I have never considered myself sexist, one of my girlfriends, who only has male children, complained of my lack of masculine candy; hence came the carousel-us-rex. A very male oriented carousel made from dinosaurs.

The base and top of the *ABC carousel* mold was poured in milk coating. I used a dinosaur lollipop mold, which had three different types of dinosaurs on it, and poured them in white coating tinted green. I did not use lollipop sticks, but instead, secured each dinosaur to a pretzel rod. I made leaves out of coating and arranged them on the carousel top to resemble a tree. This carousel was easy, fun to make and is great for a boys birthday party.

Imagine This

When you want a carousel for a special occasion, imagine the person you are making it for. Think of their favorite color, activity, hobby, or thing that makes them unique, then incorporate it into a carousel designed especially for them.

For a New Years celebration, you can make chocolate cones using the technique from Chapter 5, *The Glory of Garnishing*. Arrange them on the top of the carousel like noise makers or horns. Use ribbon or licorice laces as streamers and non-pareils or candy confetti as confetti.

You can be really creative for weddings, engagements, and anniversaries. Roses and swans always works for these special occasions. In choosing colors, incorporate the colors of the wedding party or use silver or gold dragees to acknowledge a twenty-fifth or fiftieth anniversary. Make chocolate cones in white coating filled with candy presents or flowers and arrange them on the top of the carousel.

Say it With Flowers

Flowers can and are used for every occasion. A wonderful way to combine a centerpiece and party favor is with a bouquet of candy flowers. I've made this arrangement from weddings to over-the-hill birthday celebrations; it works for all occasions simply by changing the flower, color or fabric.

You need a 3-dimensional flower mold, I prefer to use a rose, but any will work, round pieces of tulle, a container and either florist foam or styrofoam. The size of your container and the amount of tables and/or guests will determine how many flowers you will need. Make the determined amount of 3-dimensional flowers in your desired color and place each one in the appropriate sized polypropylene or cellophane bag (refer to Chapter 9, *The Finishing Touches*) and set aside. It is easier but more costly to purchase pre-cut round pieces of tulle. They usually come twenty-five to a package

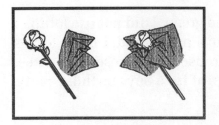

and are available in a variety of sizes, colors and patterns. They can be purchased in most craft, fabric or wedding supply stores. Fold a piece of tulle in half to form a half moon with the straight edge pointing down. Gather the straight edge together with your hands and fold around the lollipop stick. Tie a curling ribbon around the stick making sure the bag and tulle are secure. Take the styrofoam or florist foam and secure it to the inside bottom of your container (use hot glue gun or tacky tape). Insert the lollipop stick into the styrofoam and evenly arrange your flowers in the container. You can fill any bald spots by insert a gathered piece of tulle wrapped around a lollipop stick.

Coffee Time

When I was a small girl, almost everyday, my Mom's girlfriends would stop by the house and share a cup of coffee, cake, and good old conversation. A special closeness that women shared, that today we don't seem to have much time for. My sister Mariette (the only member of my family still living on the Island) and I have our own variation of this tradition. We try to get together as often as possible to chit-chat, and when we can't... she'll make a cup of tea, I a cup of coffee and we sip and chit-chat via the phone.

A special treat, for those special times when you can actually sit down with friends over a cup of coffee, is chocolate spoons. You can make these ahead of time and store them, so you know you will have them on hand. Take a plastic spoon and dip the bowl end into your coating and let set. After it has set, repeat this procedure, this time making sure the bowl remains filled with coating. You can also flavor the coating to make chocolate mint, chocolate raspberry, or any other delectable flavor. Wrap the bowl of the spoon in a small bag, tie it securely and store in an air tight container until needed. To use, just stir your hot coffee with the spoon and

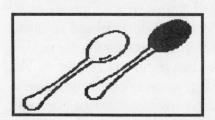

allow the hot coffee to melt the chocolate. Chocolate spoons add a special touch to dinner parties, showers, weddings and any other occasion where coffee is served.

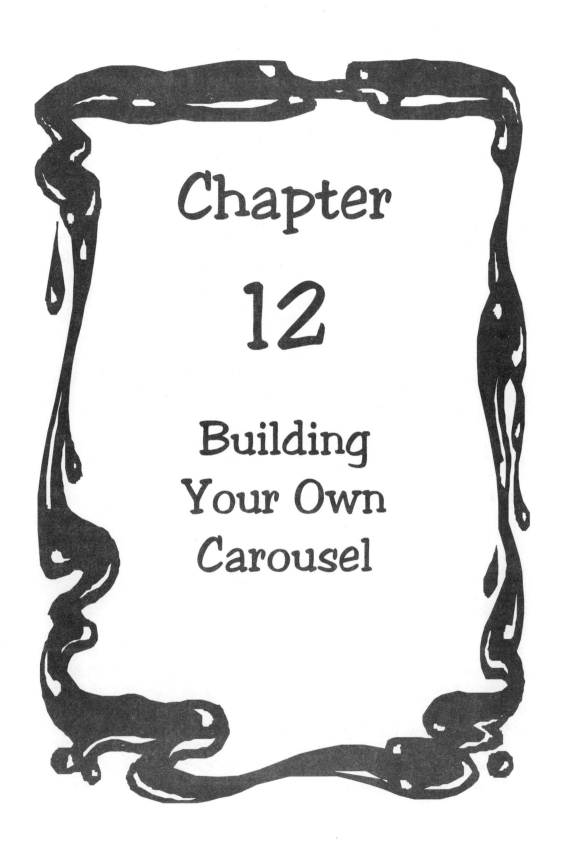

Chapter

12

Building
Your Own
Carousel

The Carousel

...Big birds and singing mice; secret gardens and carousels; painted ponies who went round and round in pastel colors, up and down . . . You've learned all the tips, tricks and shortcuts that I learned through my years of chocolate making; you've taken a ride on my carousel; now it's time you conjure up that childhood sense of magic you possess and create your own carousel.

The Journey

We now journey back to the day the carousel pictured on the front cover of this book was made. Reproducing the carousel step-by-step, I explain in detail, what inspired me to make this particular carousel, every item used to make it, even the difficulties I encountered. Armed with your new knowledge of techniques and special effects, you can reproduce this carousel or substitute any item and build a carousel unique in design, to fit your own sense of magic and childhood memories.

The carousel on the front cover of this book was not the original one planned. The original design was an old fashioned carousel with several different animals on it. I had painstakingly worked out every detail, measured every amount, had all the required molds, was making it in dark chocolate . . . and hated it. So, I started over from scratch . . . and with a deadline. My photo shoot was planned for the very next day. Believe me when I tell you, I literally winged it until I was satisfied. Which just goes to prove my point, with a little imagination you can take an idea and things you have around the house and create a spectacular piece.

The Inspiration

In all honesty, I did use a few items that were planned for the original carousel . . . the hexagon pan; everything else I used came from Stephen's kitchen or the shelves of my candy room. I started out with dark coating and switched to white. I must have been PMSing, feeling like a mush and being sentimental because the white coating, reminded me of romance and weddings, which, in turn, inspired a romantic theme. I visualized a carousel that could be set on top of a wedding cake and proceeded to reproduce my thoughts on a much larger scale and in coating. In my excitement, as I created, I forgot to weigh out each individual piece; the weights are some what accurate, give or take an ounce. The following list describes the items used, quantities, dimensions, and (approximate) weights. The one weight I am sure of is the final one, which was 19¾-pounds. The carousel stood 19½-inches tall, 15½-inches wide, and 13½-inches deep.

THE TOP: ¼-inch deep x 15-inch hexagon, 1½ lbs.

FILIGREE TRIANGLES: Twelve 7x7x4½ triangles, 1 oz. each

THE BOTTOM: ½-inch deep x 15-inch hexagon, 3 lbs.

3-D ROSES: *Life of the Party* #F-15 mold, seven pieces, 1¼ oz. each

POLE: 3½-inch wide x 2¾ deep x 13½ tall, used a plastic rose box 19½-inches long, 6 pieces, 9 oz. each

FENCE: *Life of the Party* #M-50 mold, 12 pieces, ½ oz. each

SWANS: *Life of the Party* #W-20 mold, 3 pieces, ½ lb.

SUGAR ROSES: 23 pieces

PEPPERMINT STICKS: 3 white

GOLD PETAL DUST

OPALESCENT DUST

LARGE GOLD DRAGEES: 256; 32 front; 32 back; 192 fence

SUGAR CRYSTALS

VAN LEER'S VANILLA SNAPS

15-INCH HEXAGON-SHAPED CAKE PAN

The Top

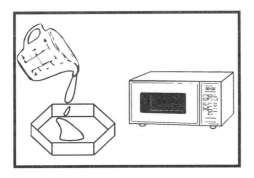

After filling my measuring cup to the brim with white coating, I melted it in the microwave and then poured the coating directly into the hexagon pan. I placed the pan in the refrigerator to set. While I was waiting for the coating to set, using the technique from Chapter 5 *The Glory of Garnishing,* I cut a long

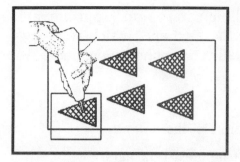

piece of waxed paper and placed it on my counter. I had a template already made for the filigree top pieces (an idea inspired from a music box made by Enesco®) and placed it under the paper so I could pipe the twelve pieces needed for the top. My husband Stephen walked in at that moment and being a skeptic, announced "I don't think you are going to be able to remove them without breaking them." NOTE: Filigree pieces are delicate, so it is wise to make one or two extra, however, to Stephen's surprise, they did come off the waxed paper easily (I only cracked one), just be gentle.

When the top was set, I inverted the pan, keeping my hand pressed against the coating so it would not crack when it popped out of the pan. It released without a hitch, was smooth and shiny. Now the trick was to get the filigree pieces on the top. Before I started this task, I melted and poured my coating into the hexagon pan to make the bottom and placed the pan in the refrigerator to set.

Assembeling The Filigree Sections

The filigree pieces attach to each other at such an angle, you wish that you had three hands, since we don't, assemble them together in the following manner. Make a copy of the "third hand" template from the template section of this book and place it on the counter. Position one filigree piece on the left line and support it with a cup or small jar. Do the same for the right side. Carefully pipe a thin line of coating on the top, using only enough coating to hold it together. After it has set, gently turn the section on its side, use the cup or jar for support and pipe a thick line of coating on the

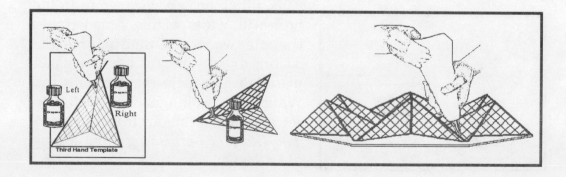

inside to secure the two pieces. After you have assembled all six sections, carefully place them on the top piece. Do not secure them to the top until you have them all positioned. Pipe a thin line of coating in between the sections to secure them.

The Center Support Pole

Finding something to use as the support pole in the center of such a large carousel was a challenge. No mold in my entire collection was wide or tall enough. I pondered. Then I noticed my plastic rose boxes left over from Valentine's Day; they were long, flexible and would probably do the trick. I filled one with melted coating and let it set, the molded piece came out of the box with ease, but wasn't quite wide enough. So, I tried it again, but this time, filling two boxes half full. After they had set, I positioned them side by side, which would give me the width I was looking for but not the depth. I made four more pieces. I reasoned if I placed two pieces together to form the front and did the same for the back, I would have the width, and one on each side would give me the depth. I used the "box" technique from chapter 7, *Incredible Edible Containers*. I placed the two front pieces together and piped a thick line of coating to join them together. It worked but was not that attractive. Looking around the room (quickly before the coating set) I saw a jar of gold dragees that were leftover "buttons" from the Nutcracker soldiers I had made the year before, I quickly placed the dragees in the line of coating. I did the same for the back section and then secured all four sides to form a rather tall box.

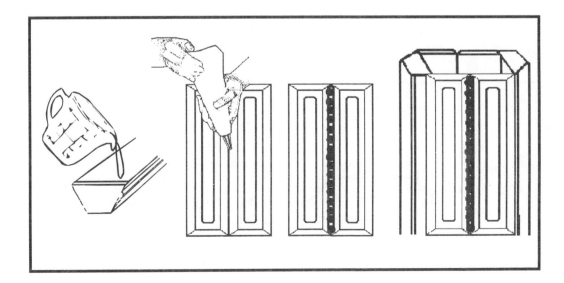

Assembeling The Top and Bottom

The next step was to secure the center piece to the bottom, which proved to be a snap. I positioned it, and then poured about a quarter cup of melted coating down the center piece "box." After the coating was completely set, I piped some coating around the rim of the top of the center piece and gently positioned the filigreed top onto it. Standing back from the counter, I was psyched! I just love it when a plan comes together!

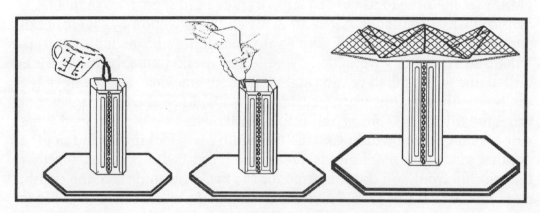

Bordering The Bottom

The top of the carousel and the center were covered with decorations which made the bottom look bare in comparison. I wanted to add something to spruce it up a bit without detracting from the top or making it too gaudy, a simple border I thought. I had an accessory mold that I liked to use to complement a house that I frequently make, so I took it out. It was just the right height and only a few pickets (the individual sticks on a fence that make up a section) from each section had to be trimmed to make it fit around the bottom. I made twelve sections and positioned them around the perimeter of the bottom piece. Since I had accented the top and center pieces with gold, I decided to follow through and add a gold accent to the bottom. After brushing the fences

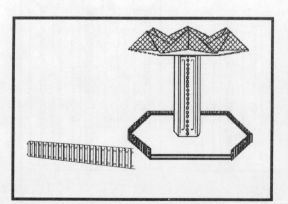

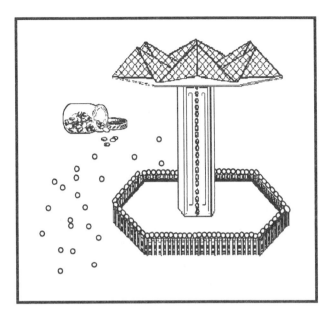

with the gold dust, I knocked over the bottle of dragees (I should follow my own advice and put things away after I use them). Little gold balls rolled everywhere, and a few balls rolled over to the top of a fence section...and the idea for placing a dragee on the top of each picket was born. I sat there like a twit putting a dab of coating on each picket and placing a hundred and ninety-two tiny gold balls on top. It really wasn't tough, after all, I had my cup of French Vanilla Cafe and was singing along (3-D above pain) to my back-to-the-seventies-CDs. After a chorus of *Anticipation* the fence was attached to the bottom with several dabs of melted coating.

The Swans

There was no question about it, a carousel like this required swans; so into the wedding molds I went and emerged with *Life of the Party's* swan. Holding the mold against the carousel, three swans became the desired amount. Since the swan was a closed ended 3-dimensional mold, I used method one for making a semisolid piece from Chapter 4, *Making Molded Magic.* The way the swans head was positioned, was reminiscent of *The Swan Princess*, and what does every princess need? A crown. While looking around my candy room for something to use as a crown, I remembered I had purchased a box of 24 white sugar roses for a project I had planned to make and never did. They were small enough but I had to trim the bottoms straight across so they would lie flat on the swans' head. The roses were bright white in color and stood out against the ivory white color of the coating; I dusted them with gold petal dust and they sparkled like the crowns they were meant to be. I crowned each swan using a dab of melted coating.

The Roses

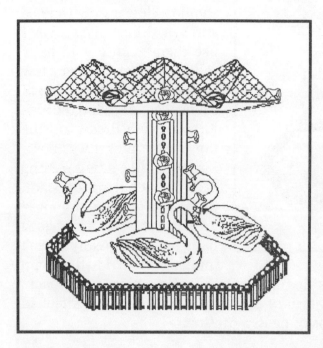

Not wanting the other 21 roses to go to waste, I brushed each one with gold dust and placed them in the corners of the filigree sections…now the center piece looked naked! So, I attached four roses on the front and the back, and then three on each side. The carousel was coming alive. I thought about putting a rose inside each filigree section but only had one sugar rose left. I went back into the wedding molds and emerged with *Life of the Party's #F-15, 3-dimensional rose mold* . I made seven roses; one for inside each section and one for the top, brushing them with gold dust before attaching them. Something was missing, but what? The carousel was beautiful…the poles! The swans were sitting there as if swimming on a pond, but there were no poles to show that it was indeed a carousel.

Making it a Carousel

Scouring my shelves, I decided to use peppermint sticks, after all I had hundreds of them in all sizes and colors. I chose three white ones, but they looked stupid sitting on the swan and then abruptly ending, they needed a ball at the end. I tried dragees, too small; I tried gum balls, too big; what if I dipped the end in coating? Taking the end of the stick, I dipped just the tip into melted coating and let it set. I repeated the process again but before the coating set, I rolled the tip in a dish of coarse sugar crystals, and then attached the peppermint sticks onto the back of the swans with a dab of coating. As a final touch, I brushed the wings of each swan with opalescent petal dust and the carousel was complete.

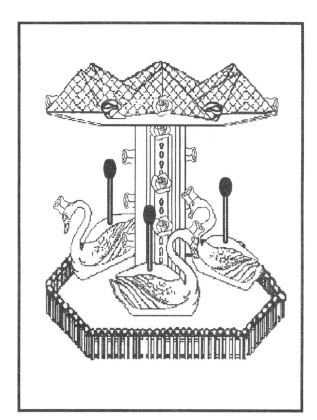

All my friends came over to see "the carousel," and everyone was promised a piece of candy to take home after the photo shoot. Naturally, everyone wanted the carousel, which left me with the final dilemma of whom to give it too.

At the studio, the carousel was the first piece of candy to be photographed. Afraid that it might get broken, we placed it in the back of the van to keep it safe. It was a hot sunny day... it just melted away...

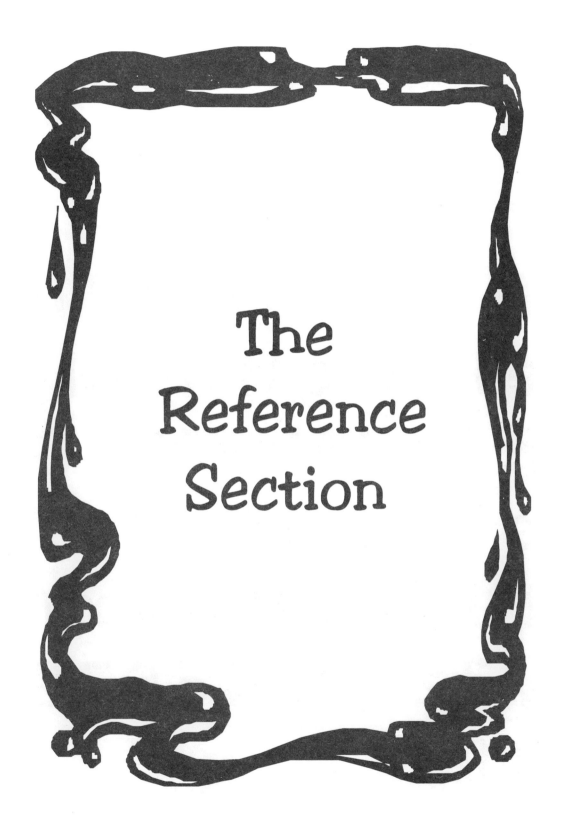

The
Reference
Section

Templates

On the following pages are templates for your use. It is easier, and less messy, to make a photocopy of the picture you want to use instead of trying to use them straight from the book. Many photocopy machines are able to enlarge or shrink the image, which is less frustrating than trying to reproduce something freehand.

Piping letters & Numbers

A a B b C c D d E
e F f G g H h I i J j
K k L l M m N n O
o P p Q q R r S s T
t U u V v W w X x Y
y Z z 1 2 3 4 5 6 7 8
9 0

Ornamental Piping

Flower Petals

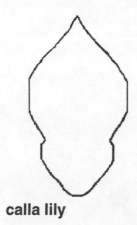

calla lily

Large, medium and small rose petal

Filigree Top & Third Hand

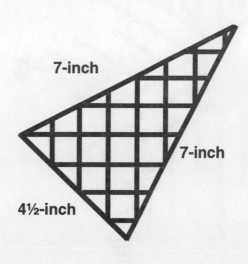

7-inch

7-inch

4½-inch

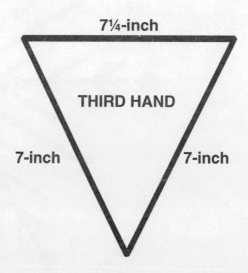

7¼-inch

THIRD HAND

7-inch

7-inch

Boxes & Blocks

The six pieces below are sized to fit each other. They can be used as is or you can enlarge them on a photocopy machine. To ensure your dimensions are accurate, make a copy of the whole page; then enlarge each piece individually, using the same magnification number.

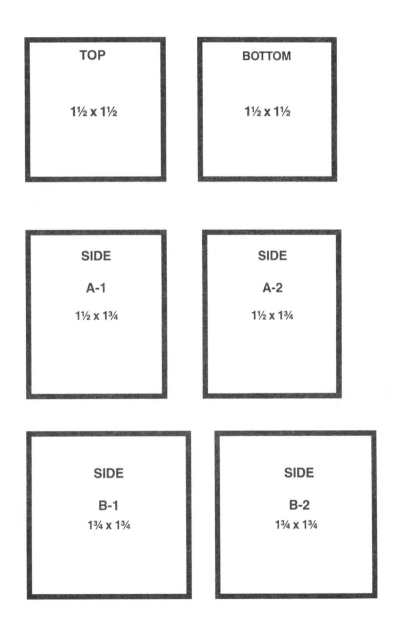

A Nice House

The pieces of this house are drawn to fit together as is, providing you want a small house. The dimensions given on the sides, are provided if you wish to have a bigger house. You can photocopy each section, using the same magification for each, to make the biggest or smallest house you wish. After you have built your house, remember to pipe windows, doors and other accessories onto it.

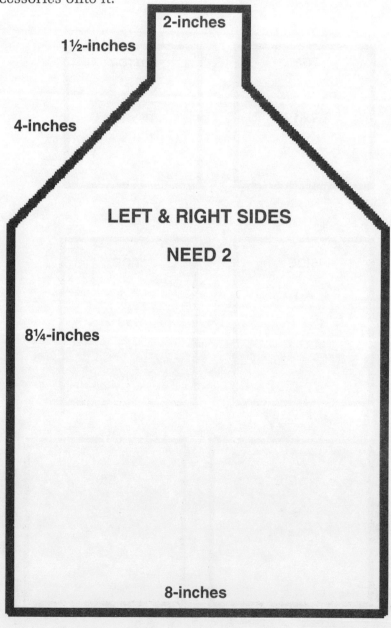

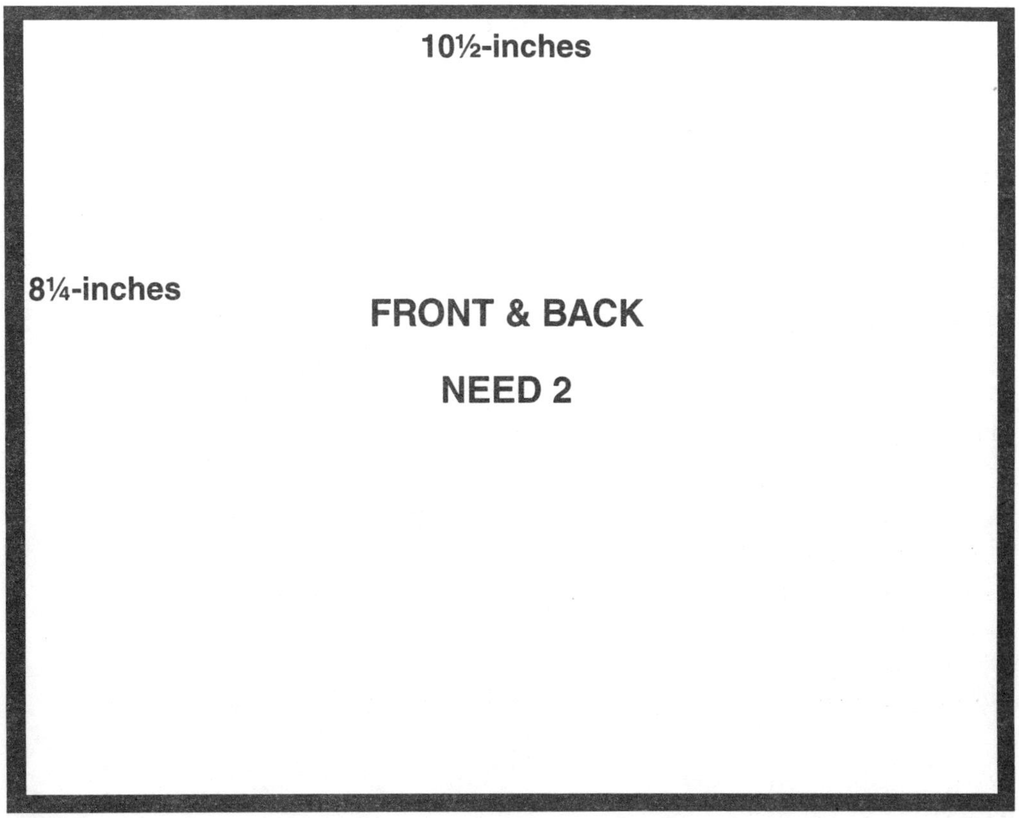

10½-inches

8¼-inches

FRONT & BACK

NEED 2

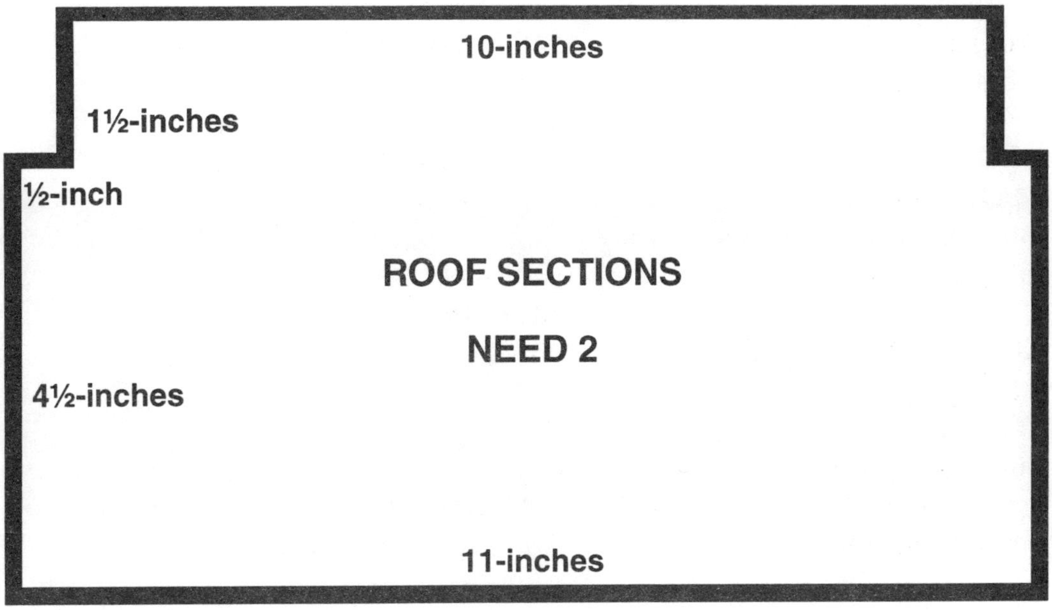

10-inches

1½-inches

½-inch

ROOF SECTIONS

NEED 2

4½-inches

11-inches

Coating Manufacturers

Remember, unless they have a retail outlet, manufacturers do not sell to individuals; call the manufacturer for a supply store in your area that carries their line of products. For imported coatings, refer to the section of specialty stores. Don't forget to mention you learned about their product from *The Chocolate Carousel.*

AMBROSIA/GRACE COCOA
12500 West Carmen Avenue
Milwaukee, WI 53225
(414) 358-5700
1-800-AMBROSIA (262-7674)

BLOMMER Chocolate Company
1101 Blommer Drive
East Greenville, PA 18041
(215) 679-4472
1-800-825-8181

CARMA Chocolate
Albert Uster Imports, Inc.
9211 Gaither Road
Gaithersburg, MD 20877-1419
(301) 258-7350
1-800-231-8154

GHIRARDELLI Chocolate
1111-139th Avenue
San Leandro, CA 94578
(510) 297-2625

GUITTARD Chocolate
10 Guittard Road
P.O. Box 4308
Burlingame, CA 94010
(415) 697-4427
1-800-468-2462

HAWAIIAN VINTAGE CHOCOLATE
461 Kilauea Avenue Suite 435
Honolulu, Hawaii 96816
(808) 735-8494

MERKENS Chocolate
150 Oakland Street
Mansfield, MA 02048
1-800-637-2536

PETER'S Chocolate/Nestlé
800 North Brand Boulevard
Glendale, CA 91203
1-800-368-5594

VAN LEER Chocolate
110 Hoboken Avenue
P.O. Box 2006
Jersey City, NJ 07303-2006
(201) 798-8080
1-800-VAN-CHOC

WILBUR Chocolate
20 North Broad Street
Lititz, PA 17543
(717) 626-1131

WILTON
2240 West 75th Street
Woodridge, IL 60517
1-800-772-7111

Specialty & Supply Stores

Below is a list of specialty and supply stores that I have become aquainted with. Everyone listed has always been very nice and helpful.

ALBERT USTER IMPORTS
9211 Gaither Road
Gaithersburg, MD 20877
1-800-231-8153
Carma, Bombasei Transfer
Sheets plus a wide variety of
confectionery products

ASSOULINE AND TING
314 Brown Street
Philidelphia, PA 19123
215-627-3000
1-800-521-4491
Valrhona plus other confectionery and gourmet products

EMILY'S CHOCOLATE STORE
204 Smithtown Boulevard
Nesconset, NY 11767
516-265-8960
Merkens, Nestlé and a full line
of candy supplies

GOURMAIL
126A Pleasant Valley St. #401
Methuen, MA 01844
Cacao Barry, Callebaut & Peter's

KERRIE'S KANDIES
2160 Route 112
Coram, NY 11727
516-696-4947
1-888-745-2634
Wilbur, Merkens plus a full line
of candy supplies

KITCHEN KRAFTS
P.O. Box 442
Waukon, IA 52172-0442
1-800-776-0575
Quality foodcrafting equipment and
supplies

LA CUISINE
323 Cameron Street
Alexandria, VA 22314
703-836-4435
1-800-521-1176
Valrhona plus gourmet cooking supplies

PARADIGM
5775 SW Jean Road, Suite 106A
Lake Oswego, OR 97035
1-800-234-0250
Ghirardelli, Guittard, Lindt, Merkens
and Peter's

PATCHOGUE FLORAL
10 Robinson Avenue
Patchogue, NY 11772
516-475-2059
Ribbons, Boxes and Cellophane bags

ROSIE'S CAKE & CANDY CLOSET
40 McDermott Avenue
Riverhead, NY 11960
516-727-8965
516-369-3507 FAX
Van Leer, Merkens plus a full line of
candy supplies

Mold Manufacturers

Unless a manufacturer has a retail outlet, they use a distributor to sell their molds. Call for the name of a specialty or supply store in your area.

CLASSIC DESIGN MOLD
751-16 Koehler Avenue
Ronkonkoma, NY 11779
516-471-5374

EAST COAST MOLD
69A Nancy Street
West Babylon, NY 11704
516-253-2397

LIFE OF THE PARTY
832 Ridgewood Avenue
Building #2
North Brunswick, NJ 08902
732-828-0886
908-828-0886 FAX

TOMRIC
136 Broadway
Buffalo, NY 14203
716-854-6050

Tempering Machine Manufacturers

ACMC
3194 Lawson Boulevard
Oceanside, NY 11572
516-766-1414

CHANDRÉ LLC
14 Catharine Street
Poughkeepsie, NY 12601
1-800-3-CHOCLA (324-6252)

HILLIARD'S CHOCOLATE SYSTEM
275 East Center Street
West Bridgewater, MA 02379-1813
508-587-3666

Index

Did you borrow this book?
Would you like a personalized autographed copy of your own or perhaps for a friend?

It's really simple. Please do not tear out this page, we will be happy to deduct .25¢ for a photocopy. Fill in the information below and we will send your AUTOGRAPHED copy right to you.

PLEASE TYPE OR PRINT ALL INFORMATION

NAME TO APPEAR IN BOOK:_____

PURCHASER'S INFORMATION

NAME: _____

ADDRESS:_____

CITY:_____ STATE:_____ ZIP:_____

SENT TO INFORMATION (IF DIFFERENT FROM PURCHASER)

NAME: _____

ADDRESS: _____

CITY: _____ STATE: _____ZIP: _____

For Each Book enclose: $19.95 plus

SALES TAX:

Please add 8.25% for books shipped to New York addresses.

SHIPPING:

Book Rate: $3.50 for the first book and $1.25 for each additional book (Surface shipping may take three to four weeks)
Overnight or Express shipping: call for quote
DISCOUNT: .25¢ FOR PHOTOCOPY

MAIL TO:
SCRATCH & SCRIBBLE PRESS
P.O. BOX 490
RIDGE, NY 11961
516-345-5463

DO YOU WANT TO BE ON OUR MAILING LIST? YES   NO